BOOKS

* * *
ESSENTIAL

[handtools]

26

tools to renovate and repair your home

[contents]

THIS OLD HOUSE ®
ESSENTIAL HAND TOOLS,
A *THIS OLD HOUSE* ® BOOK
BY THE EDITORS OF
THIS OLD HOUSE MAGAZINE

PRINTED IN THE UNITED
STATES OF AMERICA
NEW YORK, NEW YORK

FIRST EDITION
ISBN 0-9666753-0-4

10 9 8 7 6 5 4 3 2 1

COVER PHOTOGRAPHY:
JIM COOPER

Library of Congress Cataloging-in-Publication Data
This old house essential hand tools.   26 essential tools to renovate and repair your home.
          p.   cm.
          ISBN 0-9666753-0-4 (alk. paper)
          1. Dwellings—Maintenance and repair—Equipment and supplies.
2. Tools.   I. This old house.
TH4817. T49   1998   98-41705
643' .7—dc21

***

ASK A craftsman and YOU'LL FIND THAT ALMOST EVERY ONE WILL PROFESS A LOVE OF HAND TOOLS. WHAT'S MORE, the explanation THAT

FOLLOWS INVARIABLY TURNS TRADESMEN INTO POETS. TOM SILVA, contractor for *This Old House*, puts it this way: "If you've ever trued up a door with a long door plane and heard it slice off the wood, there's nothing nicer than hearing that sound or smelling the wood and feeling the shavings curl up on your arms." Hand tools are elegantly simple and peaceful to use;

they are the sail to the outboard of power tools. Using them isn't necessarily better than working with power tools; it's just different. But what a difference. ✳✳✳ As master carpenter for the celebrated television series *This Old House*, Norm Abram introduced the notion of building craftsmanship to millions of people. (How did he earn the title "master carpenter," you ask? Doing roughly 30 years of serious on-the-job carpentry.) And Tom, as a busy construction and remodeling pro, has seen more parts of more houses than you can imagine. Norm and Tom love what they do, and most of what they do involves tools. As Norm once noted, "Hand tools largely defined my father's career, and mastering them is how I began." ✳✳✳ When Norm worked on his first projects as a teenager, house building was a craft still practiced by those who, like his father, Louis, built with handsaws and hammers. Tools were cradled in fabric loops sewn to a carpenter's overalls. Experience was earned by working with seasoned craftsmen. These days, construction is a split-second world of power planes, laser levels and the arterial links of power cords. Norm wouldn't build without power tools, of course, but he brings to his work a sense of tradition and a level of craftsmanship that comes from years of reliance on hand tools. Tom puts it this way: "We used to make our own miter boxes, but my nephew Charlie has known mostly power tools. I don't think he's better or less of a craftsman, but he'll never get that feeling that comes from working primarily with hand tools." ✳✳✳ In the following pages, drawn from *This Old House* magazine, you'll pick up practical tips for the use and care of hand tools directly from Norm, Tom and other craftsmen. The surface of a favored tool, paint-flecked or burnished smooth from years of use, reminds us of what a craftsman—or an amateur—can accomplish. With any luck, it may even represent the cherished and irreplaceable, such as the block plane that Norm inherited from Louis. Tools with that kind of connection bring more to the work than a keen edge.

—THE EDITORS

[**blockplanes**]

NORM ABRAM DIDN'T PAY much attention to the block plane that came in the Handy Andy toolbox he was given at age 6. But by the time he was 15, "close enough to an adult to look like I belonged on a job," he had begun to realize how indispensable the tool could be. Working as his father's apprentice during school vacations, Norm pulled out the plane whenever he had to shrink a piece of wood just a bit, whether closing up a gap in a miter joint or squaring up a shingle. Then he discovered the low-angle block plane (right), a sleeker model with a blade that is angled just 12 degrees up from the sole (instead of the usual 20 degrees) to reduce the chance of ripping deep into the wood. Norm kept his old block plane, but these days he uses only the low-angle plane: "I like the size of it. It slides easily into my tool belt and fits my hand comfortably so that I can hold a piece of material with one hand and plane it with the other." Number one on Norm's list of uses for a block plane is trimming siding shingles, but it's every bit as useful for working the edges of furniture or fine-tuning the fussy miters of window and door trim.

Some woodworkers revere their planes, waxing and buffing them until they shine, and generally treating them more like sacred objects than like the working tools they were originally manufactured to be. Not Norm. His 25-year-old low-angle block plane reveals itself as a true carpenter's tool. It's pitted from being used out-of-doors, even though he periodically uses steel wool to buff off rust. The sole is nicked from hidden nails he has hit, and it's cracked from having been accidentally dropped. It's in such bad shape that at one point he started using his father's old plane, which he found while rummaging through a tool box. Even with Norm's large inventory of power tools, he still considers this plane his tool of choice for many trimming and smoothing jobs. A tuned-up block plane cuts quickly and accurately, though rushing into action without testing the plane on scrap can easily ruin the wood. Norm always uses scrap material to test the blade's sharpness, depth of cut and squareness for the kind of trimming or smoothing he wants. And when cutting softwoods he'll wipe down the blade now and then with a rag dipped in turpentine or paint thinner to remove resins that accumulate on the cutting surface. Instead of making clouds

This low-angle block plane belonged to Norm's father. Louis Abram worked first as a mechanic in a woolen mill, then became a full-time carpenter when Norm was about 7. Besides building other people's houses, Louis built the family house and summer cottage. "There wasn't anything he couldn't do," Norm says.

[block**planes**]

Number 1 On Norm's List of uses for a block plane is trimming wood shingles that are used for siding. Where shingles meet at a corner (below), Norm uses a block plane to make the edge of one shingle fit the slope of the other. Common irregularities such as out-of-square shingles are also easily remedied with the tool. Norm just shakes his head when he sees roofers working on shingles using electric sanders or grinders. "They make too much dust," he says.

Cutting A Perfect Miter isn't easy. The slightest error is doubled when the pieces are mated, and if the surface underneath isn't flat, problems multiply. To shave off excess wood, says Norm, there's not a tool that can do better than a block plane. If the gap is on the inside edge, as it usually is, the remedy is to trim a bit from the outside tips (above). He planes face to back, holding the tool on a diagonal to preserve the crisp edge. With its built-in protection against cutting too deeply, a block plane is perfect for jobs that require fine-tuning.

Norm Likes To Use a block plane to knock off sharp edges or to chamfer pieces for furniture (above), especially when working with antique wood. "It looks better than the factory-like finish you get with a router," he says. It's often quicker too. This detailing often extends into end grain, which the plane cuts handily.

the name
of the tool comes from its use in smoothing butcher's blocks; it slices easily through tough end grain.

of unhealthy sawdust, a plane produces heaping handfuls of fragrant, curly shavings. "A lot of carpenters don't use their planes anymore," Norm says. "It's a shame."

Norm doesn't bother polishing the sole of a block plane, as some do, because one nick from a nail would undo hours of work, and polishing a sole is no small undertaking. But he does polish the back of the iron near the cutting edge as well as sharpening and honing the bevel on its front. A blade sharpened only

on the bevel side will always be ragged. Norm polishes the back of the iron by holding it flat against a wet diamond stone and rubbing in a circular motion. To hone the bevel, he uses a store-bought rolling jig to hold the blade steady as he pushes it across the stone, making sure to maintain whatever angle is already on the blade. A keen edge will grab when pushed across a thumbnail even if no pressure is applied; a dull edge just skids across, the sure sign of a blade in need of attention.

parts and pieces

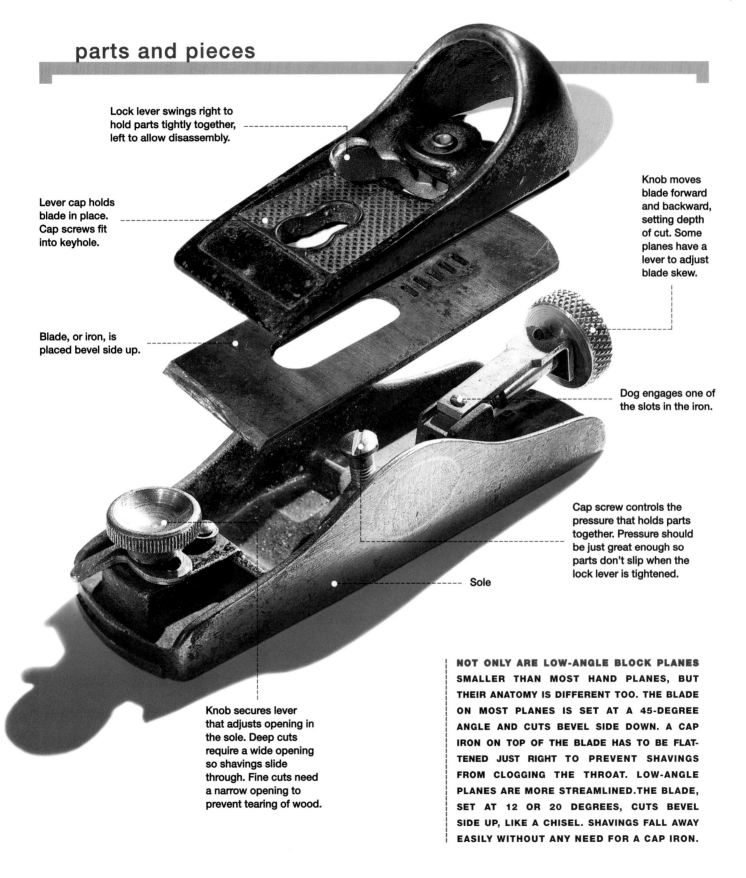

Lock lever swings right to hold parts tightly together, left to allow disassembly.

Lever cap holds blade in place. Cap screws fit into keyhole.

Blade, or iron, is placed bevel side up.

Knob moves blade forward and backward, setting depth of cut. Some planes have a lever to adjust blade skew.

Dog engages one of the slots in the iron.

Cap screw controls the pressure that holds parts together. Pressure should be just great enough so parts don't slip when the lock lever is tightened.

Sole

Knob secures lever that adjusts opening in the sole. Deep cuts require a wide opening so shavings slide through. Fine cuts need a narrow opening to prevent tearing of wood.

NOT ONLY ARE LOW-ANGLE BLOCK PLANES SMALLER THAN MOST HAND PLANES, BUT THEIR ANATOMY IS DIFFERENT TOO. THE BLADE ON MOST PLANES IS SET AT A 45-DEGREE ANGLE AND CUTS BEVEL SIDE DOWN. A CAP IRON ON TOP OF THE BLADE HAS TO BE FLATTENED JUST RIGHT TO PREVENT SHAVINGS FROM CLOGGING THE THROAT. LOW-ANGLE PLANES ARE MORE STREAMLINED. THE BLADE, SET AT 12 OR 20 DEGREES, CUTS BEVEL SIDE UP, LIKE A CHISEL. SHAVINGS FALL AWAY EASILY WITHOUT ANY NEED FOR A CAP IRON.

[chisels]

THE IDEA BEHIND A CHISEL IS STONE-AX simple—a hunk of sharp metal stuck on a handle. Perhaps that's why many are used as paint scrapers, glue chippers and can openers. Their real purpose is to cut wood: to slice tissue-thin shavings off dovetails on a drawer, or a thousandth of an inch off the tenons of a beam. No furniture maker, stair builder or timber framer could survive long without one. Neither can Norm Abram. He wraps his chisels in a canvas roll with individual pockets, keeping the edges sharp and nick-free. He uses these blades to cut mortises when hanging doors, to square up the round corners left by routers and to make cabinet dovetails. But Norm also carries a pair of utility chisels in his tool belt. There's a sharp 1-inch "stubby," which he uses for installing lock hardware, and a dull inch-wide clunker with a mediocre handle. "I use it to pry things apart and as a putty knife. It's great for scraping caulk and paint," he says.

what's sharp?
Test a chisel's keenness carefully. Gently push the edge of the chisel across a thumbnail; a dull edge will skate over the surface; a sharp one will catch.

But a beat-up chisel won't do in the workshop: "You've got to have sharp chisels for refining mortise-and-tenon joints even if you use a router. You can chisel a rounded mortise square, or you can pare a sawn tenon round so it fits the routed mortise." Norm also grabs a chisel to trim wood plugs flush or any other time there's a stray bit of wood to remove.

Good chisel technique depends on grip and body stance. A chisel should be steered with the shoulder as well as the arm but powered with the lower body. While one hand applies pressure to the handle, the other hand guides and directs. The back of the guiding hand should be braced on the workpiece, trapping the blade near the business end between index finger and thumb.

There are two basic ways to cut: vertically and horizontally. Either approach can be applied to long-grain wood surfaces as well as to end grain. Vertical paring is the power cut for slicing through a lot of wood in a hurry. The chisel's bevel should face the waste side of the cut. Rocking the chisel from side to side helps it slice tough wood.

Horizontal paring allows maximum visibility and control, which makes it perfect for fine work. The chisel is held as an extension of the forearm, pocketed into the palm, with an index finger alongside the blade. Body weight, not arm power, pushes the chisel through a cut. A timber framer or furniture maker trimming an ornery piece of oak sets his elbow in his hip and drives forward from the

Shock washer

Front face

SHEFFIELD ENGLAND
3/4"
19
mm
HAND FORGED

① ② ③

Ferrule

Bevel

Perfect Peelers:
1., 4. Whether fitted with
a handle made either of wood
or of polypropylene, modern
bench chisels (also known
as firmers) have beveled
blade edges that enable them
to reach into tight corners.
2. Carving chisels have thin
blades that taper, top and
bottom, to the keen edge
needed for working in the
round instead of on the
flat. An octagonal handle
keeps a tool from rolling
off the workbench.
3. A cranked-neck chisel
keeps the user's knuckles
out of the way when
trimming plugs on a floor or
shaving long dadoes on
a bookshelf.

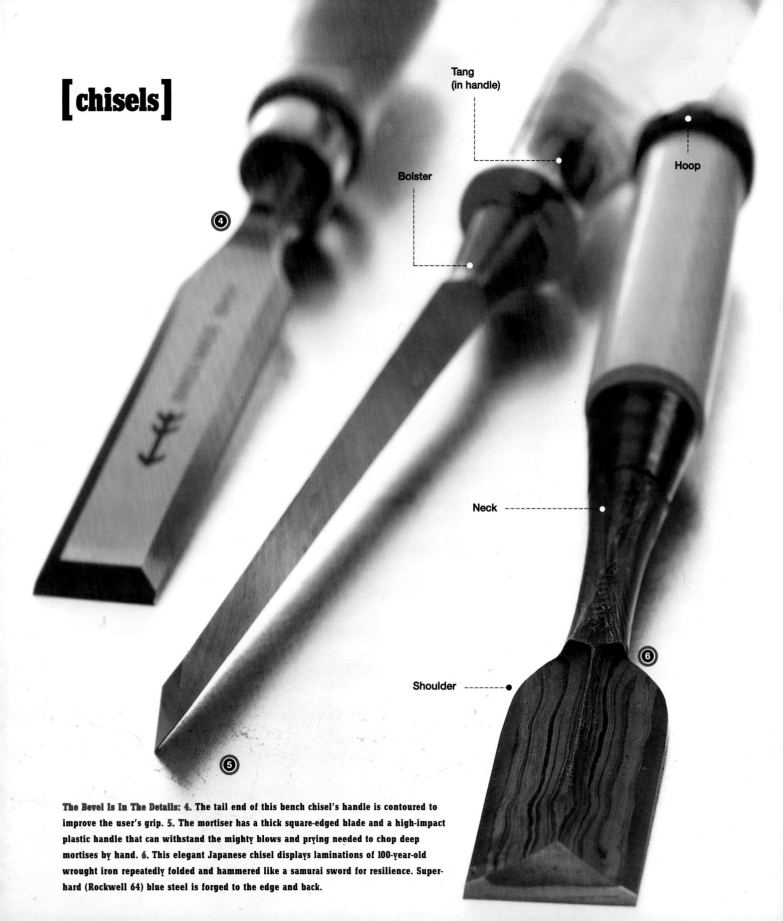

[chisels]

Tang
(in handle)

Bolster

Hoop

Neck

Shoulder

The Bevel Is In The Details: 4. The tail end of this bench chisel's handle is contoured to improve the user's grip. **5.** The mortiser has a thick square-edged blade and a high-impact plastic handle that can withstand the mighty blows and prying needed to chop deep mortises by hand. **6.** This elegant Japanese chisel displays laminations of 100-year-old wrought iron repeatedly folded and hammered like a samurai sword for resilience. Super-hard (Rockwell 64) blue steel is forged to the edge and back.

knees. For smaller, less stubborn work, Norm simply locks his elbows and leans into the cut.

A chisel is meant to take off wood in a series of slices, never a single big bite. When chiseling out a hinge mortise, for example, first make a series of shallow vertical slices; then shave them away with a horizontal cut. Likewise, cutting across end grain may splinter the back side of the wood if done too recklessly. Chisel first from one side and then from the other. Go all the way across only when shaving off the last sliver. For safety, always keep both hands behind the cutting edge, and don't hold the workpiece with one hand while whittling away with the other. If the chisel slips, it's often good-bye to some blood and tendons or a perfectly good finger.

Looking for a good chisel? The details of handle style and blade length govern what one can do. Chisel blades with single bevels and flat backs are self-jigging—the blade wants to continue riding along the flat surface it has just cut. Chisels with a bevel on both sides are for carving or lathe work, not carpentry. Wooden handles are comfortable but can split if hit too hard, and they don't always line up with the blade. Handles with metal hoops can take substantial swats from wooden mallets but not from steel hammers. Plastic handles always line up with the blade and rarely break, even when hit with a hammer. Short-bladed, stubby chisels are popular with carpenters. Furniture makers prefer longer blades for their reach. Steel in American, European and Japanese chisels is uniformly excellent, with the right hardness for sharpness and durability. Shun chisels from other places.

The Second Step is to grind the bevel using a bench grinder. This step should be repeated when an edge is blunt, nicked or chipped. Pressing lightly, quickly move the chisel across the wheel. If overheated, steel turns blue, loses its temper and won't hold an edge. The bevel angle should be about 25 degrees off the back. Use a sturdy tool rest set at the right angle or follow Norm's example (right), bracing the blade with a forefinger. The bench grinder's wheel creates a dished or hollow-ground bevel on the chisel, which makes it easy to sharpen the bevel (next step) without the need for an elaborate honing guide.

Chisels Are Great Tools when sharp but no better than putty knives when blunt. Invest in the necessary sharpening equipment, and practice using it; a chisel will repay the effort with smooth, accurate cuts. The first thing to do with a new chisel is to flatten the back face (left), something that need be done only once in the life of a tool. Lay the blade on a coarse sharpening stone and work the chisel back and forth, pressing hard, until the arced machining marks disappear. Then polish the back on a finer stone until it is mirror bright near the edge. Any sharpening station needs a selection of sharpening stones including coarse, medium and fine. Diamond stones, oilstones and Japanese waterstones all work, but waterstones offer the best edge.

Grinding Leaves a sharp but weak edge, so you must create a second sharpening bevel (left). First, place the bevel's face on a medium stone; the secret is to get your body above the action. Rock the blade to find that magic spot where front and back touch the stone. Then lift the heel a bit. Pressing firmly, work the chisel forward and back to create a beveled edge (about 35 degrees). Pause to feel for a burr on the back of the blade. Once raised, polish it off with the fine stone. Then flip the blade over and polish the back. Now go work on wood.

[combinationsquares]

USE ANY TOOL LONG ENOUGH, AND IT WILL END UP A FAVORITE: the balanced hammer, the constant tape measure or the flat bar smoothed over the years by the firm grip of callused hands. A combination square is like that. Other tools, less pretty, can mark 90-degree angles or check the tricky, often dastardly 45-degree angle. But for some, a combination square is the tool of first resort for laying out every joint from scarf to miter. A trusty square is like an old figure skater: a little stiff in the slide but still graceful.

Leroy Starrett patented the combination square in 1880, originally as a precision tool for engineers and machinists. It was quickly adopted, however, by carpenters because it's also a protractor, marking gauge, depth gauge, level and steel rule, and far more versatile than an ordinary L-shaped try square. Only a combination square can put a teeny mark between the cheeks of a gnat; just the thing for fine cabinetry work or finish trim. For measuring the depth of a dado or scribing a rabbet, no other square will work. A device of rare beauty and history, calibrated to tiny fractions of an inch, the combination square links us to a time when speed was not as important as precision and grace.

In the hands of a carpenter who knows how to use one, the tool clicks and slides like an abacus: Drawing it quickly from a tool belt, the tradesman slaps it on a mark, sets the blade and strikes off a line with consummate skill, pulls it out to tune up a table saw or uses it to lay down dead-straight pencil lines of infinite length. Unfortunately, the very moving parts that make the tool so handy also make it prone to wear under heavy use and, eventually, to inaccuracy. When your combination square goes out of square, you're just plain out of

To scribe a line along the length of a board (above), Norm slides his square along the board's edge while holding a pencil against a small notch in the end of the rule. The resulting line is straight regardless of dips or bends in the wood.

A combination square has a head (this one is machined brass) that slides along a rule (here, satin-chromed steel marked in 32nds and millimeters). A ribbed thumbscrew locks the pair together. To check the tool for accuracy, girdle a 4x4 with a pencil line: If the last line drawn meets the first dead on, the square is worth keeping.

[combinationsquares]

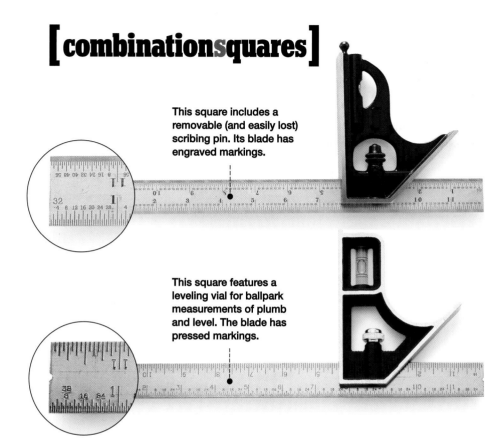

This square includes a removable (and easily lost) scribing pin. Its blade has engraved markings.

This square features a leveling vial for ballpark measurements of plumb and level. The blade has pressed markings.

Rules for this hefty cast-aluminum square come in lengths of up to 60 inches, allowing the tool to shepherd pencil lines (or saws) across plains of plywood. The head locks with one squeeze of the spring-loaded grip.

WHEN DECIDING WHICH COMBINATION SQUARE TO BUY, FIRST PICK ONE UP: THE HEAVIER THE BETTER. PLASTIC OR CAST-ZINC HEADS MAY LOSE THEIR FORM THE FIRST TIME THEY ARE DROPPED OR KNOCKED. A HEAD OF FORGED OR CAST STEEL WILL PROVIDE LONGER-LASTING STRAIGHT FACES. HOLD THE RULE UP TO THE LIGHT AND SIGHT ALONG THE EDGE. REJECT ANY WITH BOWS AND BENDS; THOSE MADE OF HARDENED AND TEMPERED STEEL WILL RETAIN THEIR SHAPE. BETTER RULES HAVE A MATTE FINISH AND MACHINE-ENGRAVED MARKINGS INJECTED WITH INK. THE ROUGH, PRESSED MARKS ON CHEAP RULES ARE LESS PRECISE AND TOUGH TO READ. FINALLY, GRAB THE SQUARE BY THE HEAD, TIGHTEN THE THUMBSCREW AND TRY TO MOVE THE RULE UP AND DOWN AND SIDE TO SIDE WITH THE OTHER HAND. ANY SLIP OR WIGGLE BETRAYS AN INACCURATE TOOL.

choosing a combination square

Protracter-Head Square: A steel rule fitted with a protractor head (below) lets Norm mark cuts for any angle from 0 to 180 degrees. He says this attachment is particularly useful to finish carpenters who frequently work with angles other than the 45 and 90 degrees of a standard square. Furniture makers prize the tool for its ability to maintain precise settings.

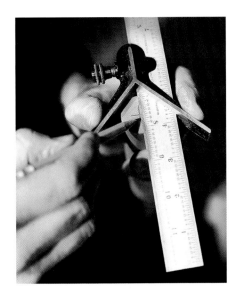

TECHNIQUES

Center-Head Square: A centering head (above) is great for finding the center of cylindrical stock; lathe workers depend heavily on the tool. Norm uses his to draw perpendicular lines across the end of the stock; where the lines intersect is the center.

Standard Square: To check the accuracy of a miter (above), Norm fits the cut between the rule and the 45-degree face of the square's head. If the miter is off, light will show between wood and rule. Carpenters also use this square to find the depth of dadoes, mortises and rabbets. By loosening the thumbscrew, slipping the rule into a dado and resting the square's 90-degree face on the wood, they get a depth reading that's more accurate than that of a tape measure.

luck. Adjustments are possible but tricky, and usually only a new square will suffice. Until about 16 years ago, most carpenters carried a combination square in their tool belts. Then one day, there's a new kid on site, carrying a clunky triangle of rustproof aluminum and zinc. He calls it a Speed Square (or a rafter-angle square), at which you sneer until you see it work. No elegance here, just blind galumphing utility. Triangular squares (huh?) make layout a breeze and, when dropped three stories onto concrete, won't loose a degree of accuracy. Yep, they're better at some jobs. But rough-and-ready simplicity won't gauge a groove or guide a pencil line to infinity or stir a carpenter's soul. For tasks such as these, only a combination square will do.

scribe a line
across a board, then flip the square and scribe another line in the same place. If the lines don't match, the square isn't accurate.

[**drywalltrowels**]

RAW DRYWALL IS NOT PRETTY. POCKMARKED WITH STAGGERED ROWS of sunken screws and scarred by a daunting gridwork of open seams covered by mesh tape, drywall stands ready to take the mud—a creamy, whitish goo otherwise known as joint compound. But after a thorough buttering with the stuff, walls and ceilings turn impeccably smooth and flat and ready to paint with no lines, lumps, bumps, dips or dimples. Somehow.

Faced with the dirty, repetitive task of making every imperfection vanish, many a drywall novice is tempted to do the same: to walk out that door and hop on a plane to Hawaii. But according to builder and remodeler Jeff Taylor, the work can be enjoyable, even inspiring (and a real picnic compared to hanging drywall). As a bonus, there's all that mud to play with. First among mud-sculpting tools, says Taylor, are the taping knives, whose metal blades range in width from 4 inches —good for deleting dimples and applying the bed coat to seams— to 2 feet—excellent for filling wide hollows or feathering out the hump of mud over butt joints. For most jobs, he uses knives with 4-, 8-, 12- and 24-inch blades.

Old-timers could sculpt inside and outside corners with only taping knives, but Taylor would be lost without his corner trowels. He has one for inside corners (think of the corners inside a box) and its mate for outside corners. Their L- shaped blades fit perfectly at wall-

ceiling junctions or over metal corner bead, leaving crisp lines and square edges.

To carry joint compound from the bucket to the wall and also to scrape excess mud off the knife, some drywallers favor the old-fashioned plasterer's hawk, a square sheet of light metal with a handle centered on the bottom. However, it takes practice to keep the

Like painters dabbing paint palettes, some drywallers use hawks (above) to keep mud at hand. A hawk should have a large surface area and not weigh too much, because it will be held for long periods. The model shown here, made of lightweight magnesium, has a 14-by-14-inch surface and a rubber handle with a soft foam disk to prevent calluses.

Smooth walls start as a windswept surf of joint compound scooped up and spread with the blue steel blade of a taping knife. Concentric circles etched into a plasterer's hawk prevent compound from slipping off the edge and, inevitably, onto boot tops.

[drywalltrowels]

to thin
mud to an easily workable consistency, add 1 cup of water per 5-gallon bucket and homogenize with a bladed paddle chucked into a hefty ¹/₂-inch drill.

hawk level; tilt it even slightly and the mud will slide off. Taylor prefers a narrow metal or plastic pan designed especially for joint compound, with a shape reminiscent of a baker's bread pan. Before going in the pan, however, the mud has to come out of the bucket. When Taylor opens a bucket, he takes the lid far away and scrapes off the mud caked on the underside. If any of these hard specks (called boogers) fall in fresh mud, they'll rake annoying grooves under a taping knife.

"Screw dimples are fun to mud," says Taylor, "but easy to miss, so I always do them first." He presses hard with a flexible 4-inch knife; one quick downward stroke fills them with mud, and a second, sideways swipe cleans any excess mud off the wall. Beginners tend to leave too much mud on dimples, which end up looking like gum wads had been stuck in rows under the paint.

Most knives have a slight bow in their blades; Taylor always puts the concave side against the wall to spread the first coat on all taped seams and dimples; mud shrinks as it dries, so this slight hump will flatten out nicely. For following coats, he uses progressively wider knives but with the convex side facing the rock to keep the tips of the blade from dragging lines in the fresh mud. When successively wider strata of mud have been built up with successively wider knives, these joints feather into sheer invisibility. Between coats, tools get scrubbed clean and wiped dry; there's nothing less conducive to good finish work than a mud-encrusted or rusty knife.

Amid the contradictions of a job in progress—glassy ceilings, pockmarked walls—mud slides easily under Taylor's knife blade, smooth as wet satin, white as milk. Soon this will all be over, and Taylor will have a lifetime supply of eminently useful plastic buckets.

choosing the right trowel

WHEN BUYING TROWELS, PAY EXTRA FOR QUALITY. A CHEAP BLADE WON'T HAVE ENOUGH FLEX, AND THE HANDLE IS ALMOST GUARANTEED TO SNAP ON THE FIRST DAY. LOOK FOR BLUE OR STAINLESS-STEEL BLADES MADE OF SPRINGY, TEMPERED STEEL, AND A COMFORTABLE, PAINTBRUSH-STYLE HANDLE OF SEALED WOOD OR CONTOURED PLASTIC FOR MOISTURE RESISTANCE AND EASY CLEANUP. FOAM OR RUBBER PADDING ON A HANDLE REDUCES THE LIKELIHOOD OF CALLUSES.

« Faced with the dirty, repetitive task of making every imperfection vanish, many a drywall novice is tempted to do the same. **»**

Trowel Talk: 1. A neoprene wipe-down knife bends to clean excess mud from inside corners wider than 90 degrees. When corners are out of reach, the knife fits on a pole. **2.** Dry, the blister brush's 9-inch-wide felt pads absorb excess water as they smooth mud. Wet, they can feather an edge almost as well as sandpaper but with no dust. **3.** With the flick of its metal lever, the adjustable neoprene round-it tool converts from a straight wipe-down knife to one for bullnose corners. **4.** A 1½-inch putty knife is handy for scraping the bottoms of mud pans. **5.** The L-shaped blades of the inside-corner trowel are angled at 103 degrees but flex to a crisp 90 degrees as the trowel is swept down a corner. **6, 7.** Taping knives, ranging from 8 to 24-inches wide, are mounted in a rigid aluminum brace to provide consistent pressure along the blade's edge. Blue steel blades are more flexible and lighter than those of carbon or stainless steel. **8.** Joint knives are the first tool used to slap the mud over a joint. They are also the narrowest (ranging from 4 to 10 inches) and the most rigid. **9.** Bowed ³/₁₆ inch in the middle, the curved-blade trowel feathers the mud to allow for shrinkage that occurs as the joint compound dries. **10.** An outside corner trowel is made with an 80-degree blade angle, but its flexible stainless-steel blade expands to 90 degrees. This one smooths bullnose corners.

[hacksaws]

They are tools of last resort.

No matter how hard the material or how desperate the situation, hacksaws refuse no challenges.

WITH THE RIGHT BLADE, ENOUGH MUSCLE AND PLENTY OF TIME, a hacksaw can slice through virtually anything: steel, brass, glass, tile, concrete, ice, bone—even stone. Their little piranha-sharp teeth never give up. Plumbers prize hacksaws for slicing through every type of pipe. Butchers use them to make short work of carcasses and frozen meat; auto mechanics rely on them to sever rusted bolts and dismember exhaust systems. Roofers trim and miter gutters with them. Though a hacksaw is hardly the handsaw of first resort for those who work wood, carpenters have been known to sneak their blades between sash and sill to free stuck windows, and nothing beats a good hacksaw blade for making a smooth cut through hardwood.

Slick as ice, this saw's unique lever system, hidden in the handle, locks in proper blade tension with a single squeeze. Spare blades are stowed in the frame's hollow rectangular bar.

Hacksaw blades come in 10- and 12-inch lengths, and some saws have adjustable frames that accommodate either size. Nonadjusting frames generally use the longer blades—they cut quicker and last longer. Blades are easy to install so there's no excuse for using a dull one. Teeth, however, should point forward, not back; the saw should cut on the push stroke.

To start a cut, score the surface of the workpiece with the edge of a file or gently drag the saw backward a couple of times. Increase pressure when the kerf is well established, but only on the push stroke or else you'll dull the teeth unnecessarily.

When Tom Silva reaches for a hacksaw, it's usually to shorten a bolt or a length of threaded rod. Before he hacks, though, he threads: By putting a nut on first and removing it *after* cutting through the bolt, he handily removes the inevitable burr of metal left by the saw. Doing otherwise almost guarantees that the shortened bolt will never mate with its nut.

[hacksaws]

This saw combines modern features like a chromed-steel tube frame and textured cast-aluminum handle with an old-fashioned blade tensioning system: a wing nut.

Mini or frameless hacksaws work well in tight quarters. Blades should be mounted to cut on the pull stroke to compensate for their lack of stiffness.

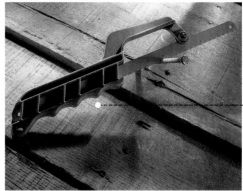

A top-mounted tensioning system combines a thumbwheel, threaded rod and an articulated lever arm to make adjustments easy. Change blades carefully: When tension is released, the pins holding the blade may fall out.

BLACKSMITHS CAME UP WITH THE IDEA FOR THE HACKSAW IN THE EARLY 1800s BY FORGING BLADES FROM BROKEN SCYTHES OR WAGON SPRINGS. FACTORY-MADE SAWS WITH WING NUTS AND STAMPED-METAL FRAMES WERE FIRST PRODUCED AFTER THE CIVIL WAR AND CHANGED LITTLE FOR MORE THAN A CENTURY. NOW SAWS HAVE RIGID TUBULAR STEEL FRAMES, CAST-ALUMINUM COMPONENTS, FRONT-END GRIPS, INTERNAL STORAGE FOR SPARE BLADES, D-HANDLES AND 45-DEGREE BLADE MOUNTS THAT MAKE ANGLED OR FLUSH CUTS EASIER. SOME FRAMES ADJUST TO ACCOMMODATE 10- OR 12-INCH BLADES; SMALL "PONY" SAWS CAN EVEN USE SCROLL-SAW BLADES.

THE BEST FEATURE OF THE NEWEST SAWS IS THEIR LEVER-ACTION TENSIONERS, WHICH CAN EASILY PUT 30,000 POUNDS OF TENSION ON A BLADE—THE OPTIMAL AMOUNT FOR FAST, STRAIGHT CUTS. OLDER STAMPED-METAL FRAMES COULD THEORETICALLY PRODUCE 15,000 POUNDS OF BLADE TENSION, BUT ONLY IF YOUR FINGERS WERE ALSO MADE OF STEEL AND MOLDED TO FIT THE PROFILE OF WING NUTS.

IN EMERGENCIES, OF COURSE, ANY OLD HACKSAW WILL DO. ONE STAFFER AT *THIS OLD HOUSE* MAGAZINE GRABBED HIS AT A MEMORABLE CHRISTMAS CELEBRATION WHEN HIS *CROQUEMBOUCHE*—STACKED CREAM PUFFS COVERED WITH CARAMEL—BECAME WELDED TOGETHER IN THE OVEN. "IT WAS NOT MY FINEST MOMENT *AU TABLE*," THE AMATEUR CHEF RECALLS SOMEWHAT SHEEPISHLY, "BUT IT WAS A CASE OF 'NO HACKSAW, NO DESSERT.'"

choosing the right hacksaw

* * *

HACKSAW BLADES

DESPITE THE ATTENTION PAID TO FRAMES, THE HEART OF A HACKSAW is its blade. The best are bimetal: a spine of flexible spring steel welded to a toothed strip of hard but brittle high-speed tool steel. Bimetals can survive modern high-tension frames; cheap carbon-steel blades will shatter easily and dull quickly. Hackers often get into trouble when they expect an all-purpose 18-teeth-per-inch blade to do everything. Such a blade works fine on nonferrous metals, metal rods and iron pipe, but on thin-walled tubing such as that used for electrical conduit, the teeth will catch, bind or even break.

Match the blade to the task, and good results are a cinch. As a rough guide, use coarse blades on thicker or softer materials, fine blades on harder or thinner ones. The coarsest blades, with 14 teeth per inch (tpi), are suitable for aluminum, plastic pipe and wood. Choose an 18-tpi blade (1, at right) to cut copper, brass and other nonferrous metals, as well as metal rods and cast-iron pipe. A 24-tpi blade (2) is best for steel conduit and sheet metal no thicker than ⁵⁄₁₆ inch. Use 32-tpi blades (3) on thin-walled tubing or sheet metal up to ⅛ inch thick, or for cutting countertop laminates or plastic. Rod and grit saws (4, 5) are the pit bulls of blades. Instead of teeth, they have superhard tungsten-carbide granules that

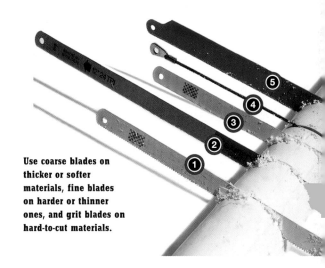

Use coarse blades on thicker or softer materials, fine blades on harder or thinner ones, and grit blades on hard-to-cut materials.

slowly grind through almost anything—brick, stone, concrete or glass. For straight cuts, use grit saws; rod saws excel at curves.

Hacksaw blades are not invincible, however. Push them too hard and they'll call it quits (left). When cutting metal, a hacksaw blade can get too hot to touch, and mistreating it just when it's working the hardest for you is one way to kill it. Don't muscle through a cut; let the tool do the work.

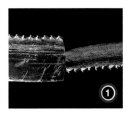 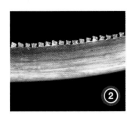 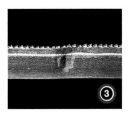

Ailing Blades: Mistreatment will ruin a blade. 1. Tightening a hot blade can make it snap in two as it cools. 2. Overheating a blade can give it a permanent bow. 3. Forcing coarse blades through hard, thin metal may break teeth. Always match the blade to the work.

[hammers]

SOMETIMES YOU HAVE TO WONDER: How does the brain do that? How can you pick up a hammer that weighs more than a pound, swing it through a huge arc at such an awesome speed you could crush the skull of an ox and then land it squarely on top of a dot of steel? That's beautiful. And it's a mighty good feeling when you do it right, says Tom Silva: "You can always tell an amateur. He doesn't swing, he tries to push the nail or punch it, he tries to do it with his wrist instead of his arm, he misses and he hits his finger. That's ugly."

« For every job that requires some sort of pummeling, there's a specific hammer that makes it easier. **»**

The family of hammers is wonderfully diverse, as evidenced by these antiques. Left to right: A mallet to work leather; a planishing hammer used by metalsmiths for smoothing surfaces; a fencing hammer; a dinging hammer for pounding out dents in sheet metal; a double-claw hammer, circa 1902, that pulls nails without bending them—the upper claw starts and the lower claw finishes the job; a bumping hammer used to remove hubcaps.

The head of a standard claw hammer can chip when used to strike steel chisels. A better choice is a hand sledge (shown here) or a ball-peen hammer; heads on these hammers are tempered to resist chipping.

[hammers]

Rip: Also known as a framer's hammer, most have a straight claw that is great for tearing up old framing or prying apart two pieces of wood to insert a wedge. The handle runs longer than others.

Rip: The head of this 22-ouncer bolts to a hickory handle for a strong connection that protects against overstrikes. One cheek is hardened for toenailing, the other is grooved for nail pulling.

Japanese Framing: A curved, cat's-paw claw provides extra nail-pulling leverage, and a nonslip rubber grip absorbs nailing shocks. Hardened bull's eyes on both cheeks allow side hammering.

by one
estimate, there are more hammer patents on the books in the United States—by far—than in any other country in the world.

A guy without several hammers is a guy without tools. Norm Abram has six quite different types in his toolbox. Tom can get by with three for general construction, but if he starts working with metal or chipping bricks, he's got to go back to the truck for more. For every job that requires some sort of pummeling, there's a specific hammer that makes it easier, safer and better done. The best ones have a forged-steel head; with cast-steel heads, tiny particles of metal tend to chip off and fly in all directions. There's also a hammer to suit nearly any personal preference for style, weight and material. When it comes to a standard carpenter's hammer, for example, Norm likes a solid-steel model with a leather-wrapped handle, but other craftsmen can't stand to swing anything but a wood-handled

Tack: Also called a cross-peen hammer, the face is good for sinking finishing nails, while the peen end is perfect for setting small fasteners such as upholstery tacks and brads.

Ball Peen: Primarily for shaping metal or driving steel cold chisels and punches. "There's nothing like it for working rivets," Norm says. Rough up a slippery wood or leather-clad handle with sandpaper.

Boat Builder's: The pointed end of the head counter-sinks fasteners. Imported from Japan, this hammer is a favorite of finish carpenters. The white-oak handle is easy on the user's hands.

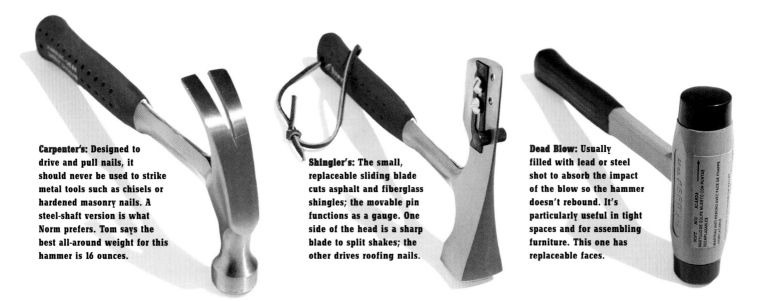

Carpenter's: Designed to drive and pull nails, it should never be used to strike metal tools such as chisels or hardened masonry nails. A steel-shaft version is what Norm prefers. Tom says the best all-around weight for this hammer is 16 ounces.

Shingler's: The small, replaceable sliding blade cuts asphalt and fiberglass shingles; the movable pin functions as a gauge. One side of the head is a sharp blade to split shakes; the other drives roofing nails.

Dead Blow: Usually filled with lead or steel shot to absorb the impact of the blow so the hammer doesn't rebound. It's particularly useful in tight spaces and for assembling furniture. This one has replaceable faces.

hammer. Steel handles have the advantage in demolition work because they're just about indestructible. In the course of a day, however, Tom switches back and forth between several hammers depending on the kind of work he has to do.

A hammer might as well be a paperweight, though, if you don't use it right. A tenpenny nail shouldn't require more than two taps to position it, then three solid blows to sink it. A common mistake the neophyte makes is to stand directly over the nail, endangering his head as he raises the hammer. Another error is gripping the hammer too close to the head. Try this: Stand back, grasp the hammer firmly near its end and swing from the shoulder instead of the elbow, in a full arc. "Above all," Norm says, "remember to keep your eye on the nail."

Barrel: A fat head puts the hammer's mass near the centerline of the handle, allowing more control when hitting chisels. Heads are tempered to be soft on the inside and hard on the outside, reducing rebound.

Split-head Rawhide: Faces of water-buffalo hide are forgiving. Used to break apart old construction when wood is to be saved or to assemble delicate items. Faces are replaceable. A favorite of timber framers.

Mallet: To many, the ultimate driver for wood-carving tools. Usually turned from a solid piece of wood. Also good for knocking wood-handled chisels and for joinery.

[**handsaws**]

WHAT POWER JUNKIES WE HAVE become, our tools tethered to an electric leash. Eyes squeezed, ears plugged, teeth clenched, we guide a screaming power saw with our fist as it devours a pencil line like a shark eating spaghetti. In the name of production, we make more cuts in less time and call it the easy way. When the cutting stops, our ears ring with the bells of progress; we spit out sawdust, breathe a sigh of relief, pull the plug and count our fingers. It might seem that anyone can master a power saw—just squeeze the trigger and shove. But working with a handsaw invites deeper awareness.

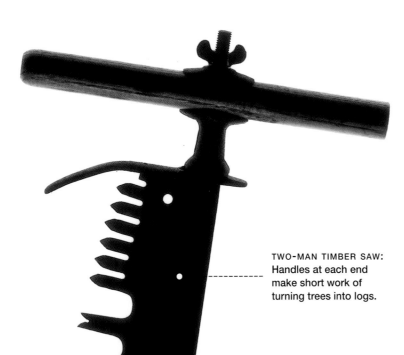

TWO-MAN TIMBER SAW: Handles at each end make short work of turning trees into logs.

Spread your wings, use good technique and you can cut nearly anything anywhere instantly, without the need for a single kilowatt. No, not whole panels of plywood. Anyone who uses a handsaw to bisect sheet stock is a Luddite. But you can hear yourself think amazing things when you cut by hand. It takes more time and skill to make straight cuts but, with practice, they become increasingly precise, and the work brings an odd serenity born of slow and conscious craft. With their ageless beauty, these tools teach a timeless lesson: Silence is peace.

Though the steel is frustratingly brittle, hand saws (above) up to 100 years old can still be sharpened and used.

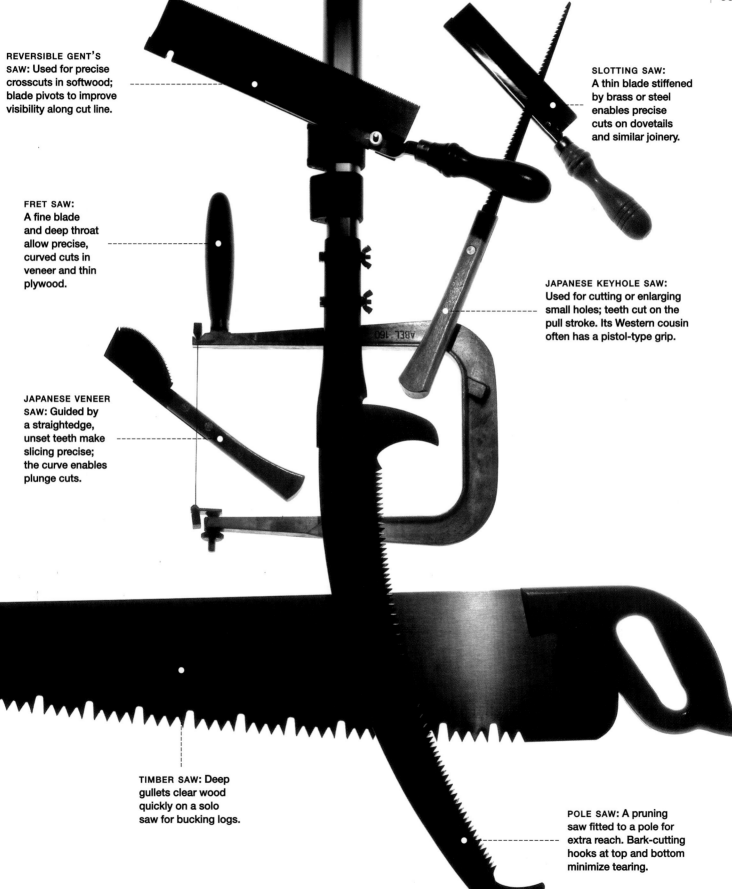

REVERSIBLE GENT'S SAW: Used for precise crosscuts in softwood; blade pivots to improve visibility along cut line.

SLOTTING SAW: A thin blade stiffened by brass or steel enables precise cuts on dovetails and similar joinery.

FRET SAW: A fine blade and deep throat allow precise, curved cuts in veneer and thin plywood.

JAPANESE KEYHOLE SAW: Used for cutting or enlarging small holes; teeth cut on the pull stroke. Its Western cousin often has a pistol-type grip.

JAPANESE VENEER SAW: Guided by a straightedge, unset teeth make slicing precise; the curve enables plunge cuts.

TIMBER SAW: Deep gullets clear wood quickly on a solo saw for bucking logs.

POLE SAW: A pruning saw fitted to a pole for extra reach. Bark-cutting hooks at top and bottom minimize tearing.

[handsaws]

Blades of Western saws are generally thicker and have coarser teeth than Japanese saws, as shown by the kerfs.

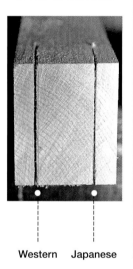

Western   Japanese

Proper technique varies with each saw, but some rules apply to all of them.

Use an upstroke to notch the wood; then stroke forward, letting the saw do the work. Don't press down. Use the entire length of the blade, not just the middle teeth. Carpenters used to tell their apprentices, "You paid for the whole saw, so cut with the whole saw." Whatever the workpiece, make sure it is securely clamped; if the wood jiggles, the cut line will be wavy. Framing lumber should always be cut on sawhorses; use your knee to hold the piece down on the trestle. Set the saw's back teeth on a layout line, and bring your arm back to make the notch, as smoothly as drawing a bow. At the same time, inhale. Your elbow should be in line with the blade at all times.

Then, your face softer than a power saw ever makes it, you shoot out from the shoulder, falling into the ancient push-and-pull rhythm that coincides with your breathing: Inhale on the back stroke, exhale on the cut—if you get dizzy, you're sawing too fast. Every three or four strokes, blow the sawdust off the cut line so you can see what you're doing.

Crosscut saws, with knifelike teeth that sever the wood fibers, are best for sizing boards to length. Ripsaws cut with the grain and at a steeper angle than crosscuts. Thanks to table saws, crosscut saws are almost obsolete; you could live all your life without ripping a board by hand. You'll probably never use a stadda saw to cut combs out of horn or a grooving saw to make dadoes in housed stair stringers or the vellum saw to fix a piano. But the compass saw, the dovetail saw, the bow saw, the fretsaw and many others are still in daily use all over the world. Introduce yourself: You can learn their ways.

* * *

JAPANESE SAWS

IF YOU STUDY THE WESTERN HAND SAW, YOU WILL SOON ENCOUNTER its cousin, the Japanese saw. The straight, swordlike handle takes a two-handed grip. Strong yet delicate, the blade cuts on the pull stroke and makes a laser-thin kerf that is perfect for fine joinery and trim. Thin blades are possible because the blade, as it cuts, is under tension rather than compression.

« Lightly running a finger along the blade of a Western saw should not cause a wound. Doing so along the teeth of a Japanese saw is much riskier. »

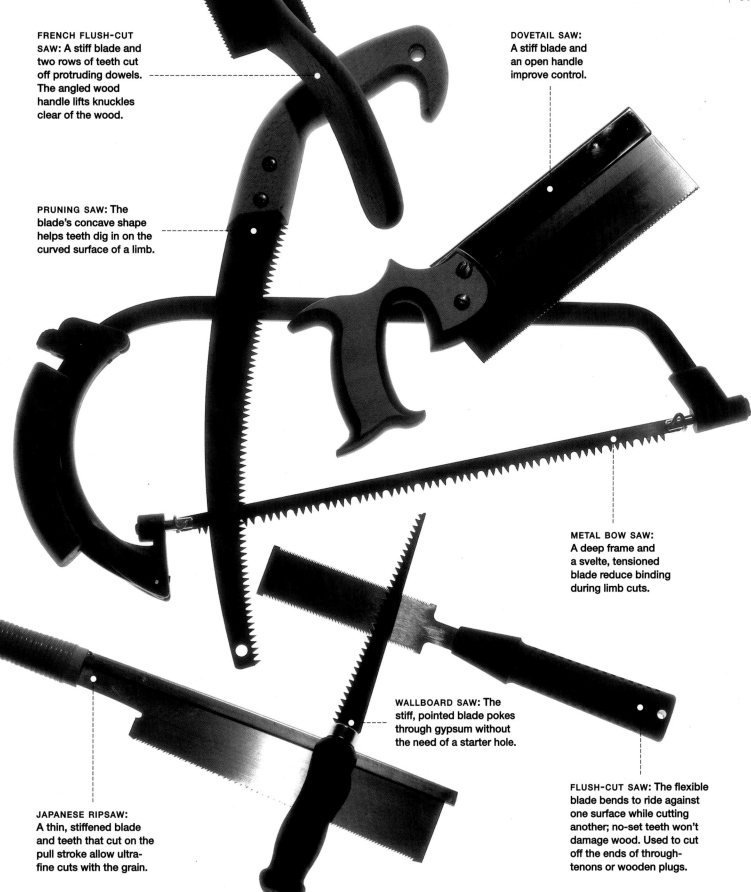

FRENCH FLUSH-CUT SAW: A stiff blade and two rows of teeth cut off protruding dowels. The angled wood handle lifts knuckles clear of the wood.

DOVETAIL SAW: A stiff blade and an open handle improve control.

PRUNING SAW: The blade's concave shape helps teeth dig in on the curved surface of a limb.

METAL BOW SAW: A deep frame and a svelte, tensioned blade reduce binding during limb cuts.

WALLBOARD SAW: The stiff, pointed blade pokes through gypsum without the need of a starter hole.

JAPANESE RIPSAW: A thin, stiffened blade and teeth that cut on the pull stroke allow ultra-fine cuts with the grain.

FLUSH-CUT SAW: The flexible blade bends to ride against one surface while cutting another; no-set teeth won't damage wood. Used to cut off the ends of through-tenons or wooden plugs.

[handsaws]

the teeth
of most saws must have the same amount of outward angle or "set," with alternating teeth pointing in opposite directions. That's so the kerf will be wider than the saw blade.

Why do Japanese saws enjoy such a loyal following, particularly given the convenience of power tools? For one thing, a pull stroke puts less stress on the blade, so Japanese saws can be made with a harder though more brittle steel. This allows for sharper teeth and a thinner blade. A thinner blade makes for an easier and finer cut because less wood is displaced. But something about the connection between a craftsman and his saw transcends other tool experiences. What makes traditional Japanese-style woodworking special is the relationship between its tools and the work they make possible. Such work often calls for intricate joinery, whether the project is a shoji screen, a garden pavilion or a modern-day palace of Japanese design. The great variety of Japanese saws means the seasoned woodworker can use just the right blade for a specific type of cut.

Using a Japanese saw takes some getting used to, however, because the entire body orientation of the carpenter is different. The low height of the Japanese-style sawhorses— 15 inches versus the 24 inches of many Western sawhorses —enables the carpenter to use his body weight for more leverage. As a result, his arms do less work.

The blades of Japanese saws generally have finer teeth than those on their Western counterparts and therefore they produce a narrower kerf. When Japanese saws are made, the heat-tempered, high-carbon steel of the blade becomes slightly thinner at the heel than at the toe, and thinner in the center than at the edges. This discourages binding. And teeth? Lightly running a finger along the blade of a Western saw should not cause a wound. Doing so along the teeth of a Japanese saw, however, would be much riskier.

TECHNIQUES

Push Stroke: The stroke of the Western ripsaw requires strength and control in one arm and puts a lot of strain on it. The craftsman's body weight is to the left of the line of cut. The result (top) is a rough cut.

Pull Stroke: The stroke of a Japanese saw takes full advantage of the user's body weight, which is above and aligned with the cut. He grips with two hands for more power and greater control. The result (top) is a smooth finish.

CROSSCUT SAW: A wide blade tracks straight despite deep cuts; the handle is equally comfortable for sawing teeth "up" or teeth "down."

COPING SAW: Used for fine curved work, as when fitting intersecting moldings to each other.

FRENCH VENEER SAW: Teeth, set on one side only, are angled so the wood can be scored with a stroke before cutting.

ENGLISH BOW SAW: The narrow blade, tensioned by a twisted cord and toggle stick, can be turned to any angle (unlike the similar woodcutter's saw).

UTILITY SAW: Versatile and compact; good for a toolbox.

JAPANESE MORTISE SAW: Useful for plunge cuts in tight spaces. Rip teeth on one side, crosscut on the other.

[**handscrapers**]

A scraper is the simplest of tools—

just a thin piece of steel with a hooked edge.

BUT THAT HOOK, PUSHED ACROSS WOOD, CAN SHAVE ROUGH SURFACES smooth in less time than a barber can clear-cut a cheek of two-day-old whiskers with a straight razor. Scraping shears wood. Sandpaper, by contrast, scours. As sanding proceeds through a series of progressively finer grits, scratches in the wood become more and more shallow until they can no longer be seen. The surface looks smooth but may feel fuzzy. A scraped board is silky; it shimmers because the wood fibers are sliced, not frayed.

The surface undulates like that of a fine antique—a reminder that before the invention of sandpaper in the late 19th century, wood was smoothed with scrapers or hand planes. Scrapers, however, cannot be used indiscriminately. Scraping softwood can crush fibers or rip them from the surface, leaving pits. But scrapers work on most hardwood, even on highly figured boards.

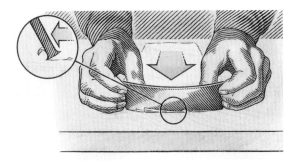

A scraper makes such a shallow cut that there's little danger of tearing hardwood fibers, regardless of which direction they face. In fact, think of a scraper as a device for removing bits of anything, and there's no limit to the jobs it can do. It can slice off brushstrokes before a final coat of paint is applied, bead a board in less time than it takes to set up a router and pare off gummy masking-tape residue. Scrapers are perfect tools for removing the washboard ripples left by the whirling knives of power jointers and planers. (If these mill marks lie at a right angle to the grain, turning the scraper at a slight skew prevents the steel from following the humps and digging deeper troughs in the wood.) Scrapers can be pulled across a surface, but most wood-workers prefer to push with their thumbs on the back of the blade, flexing it into a gentle curve. Flexing makes the blade cut at the center, not at the corners, which might gouge. A scraper should be held nearly perpendicular to the work and tilted just slightly forward. At the correct angle, it will produce lacy shavings. If the tool must be tilted so far forward that the user's knuckles drag on the wood, the hook is too large. A large hook requires complete re-sharpening more often than a small one; a small hook can be restored a dozen times with a few passes of a metal rod called a burnisher.

Sharpening a scraper is easy but unorthodox; the aim is not to create a knife edge but to fashion nearly microscopic hooks (left) on both sides of the blade. The process requires a mill file (to flatten and square the scraper edges), a sharpening stone (to smooth its sides), a burnisher (to form the hook) and a vise (to hold the scraper during preparation). It's a procedure that calls for finesse, not brawn. When a flat scraper won't fit, simply grind it down to suit the surface.

Perhaps best of all, scraping bare wood requires neither ear protection nor a respirator and even saves money. A whole package of sandpaper might be gone at the end of a single project, but an inexpensive set of rectangular and curved scrapers will last a lifetime.

Curved gooseneck scrapers can scoop out chair seats or smooth wooden bowls.

Fatiguing the scraper's edge by running a burnisher across it four times makes it more malleable. Rubbing the burnisher against the edge several times forms the hook.

[ladders]

EVER SINCE OUR ANCESTORS CLIMBED OUT of the trees, man has been a terrestrial animal. But paint peels, gutters clog, windows smear and roofs lose shingles, so we've taken to extension ladders, our portable trees, to lift us up again. Yet we can't seem to get it through our thick primate skulls that ladders, unlike trees, aren't rooted to the ground. They're portable, remember? (Perhaps the altitude turns otherwise competent people into nitwits.) In 1995, nearly 140,000 people went to emergency rooms for ladder-related injuries, an average of 383 per day. Not good.

Professionals who spend their lives aloft know that when it comes to ladders, only one thing matters: stability. All ladder wisdom flows from that point. The first bit of advice: Don't be cheap. "Buy the best you can," says Tom Silva. He uses only commercial- or industrial-grade aluminum extension ladders, though other grades are readily available.

Extension ladders come in three materials (wood, aluminum and fiberglass) and four grades (light household duty; commercial, for painters and general handymen; industrial, for contractors and maintenance workers; and professional grade, for rugged industrial and

An extension ladder should always be set against a wall, with the moving half—the fly section—on your side. A rope and pulley haul it up, and flippers (left), lock it in place. This ladder has fiberglass rails and steel rungs (right). It should be stored indoors to prevent degradation by the sun.

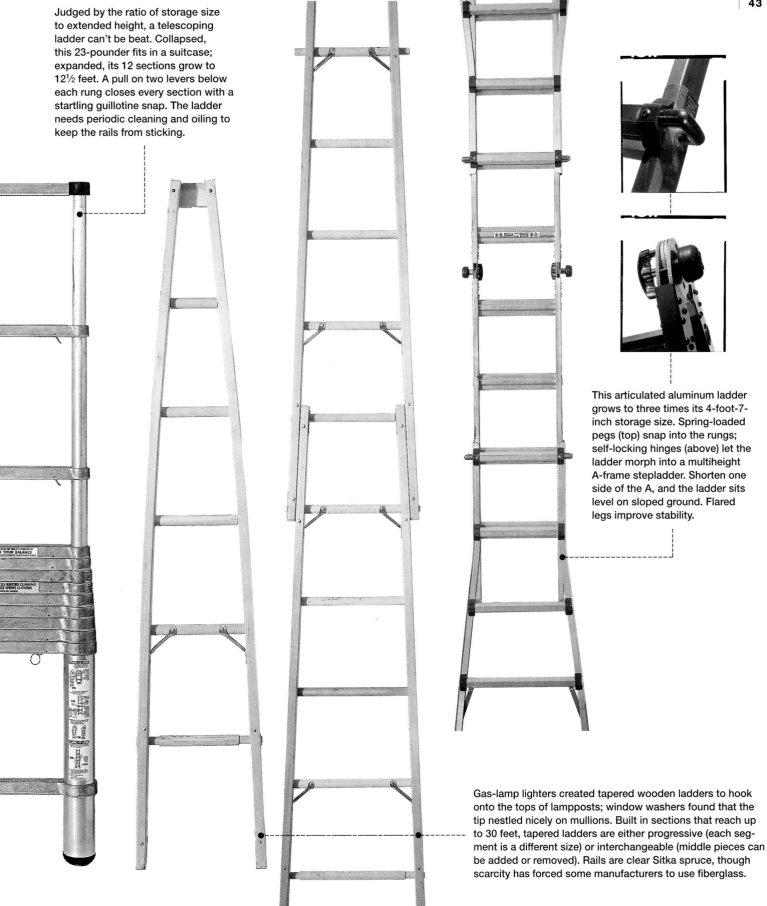

Judged by the ratio of storage size to extended height, a telescoping ladder can't be beat. Collapsed, this 23-pounder fits in a suitcase; expanded, its 12 sections grow to 12½ feet. A pull on two levers below each rung closes every section with a startling guillotine snap. The ladder needs periodic cleaning and oiling to keep the rails from sticking.

This articulated aluminum ladder grows to three times its 4-foot-7-inch storage size. Spring-loaded pegs (top) snap into the rungs; self-locking hinges (above) let the ladder morph into a multiheight A-frame stepladder. Shorten one side of the A, and the ladder sits level on sloped ground. Flared legs improve stability.

Gas-lamp lighters created tapered wooden ladders to hook onto the tops of lampposts; window washers found that the tip nestled nicely on mullions. Built in sections that reach up to 30 feet, tapered ladders are either progressive (each segment is a different size) or interchangeable (middle pieces can be added or removed). Rails are clear Sitka spruce, though scarcity has forced some manufacturers to use fiberglass.

[ladders]

fiberglass
*ladders are safer
than aluminum ladders
near wires but they
are also heavier.*

construction use). The most important difference between them is the weight they'll carry—from a 200-pound maximum for household duty to 300 pounds for professional grade.

After choosing a good extension ladder, use it well. To see how far away from the wall a ladder's feet should sit, divide its extended length by four, says John Dee, a painting contractor in Concord, Massachusetts. In other words, a 16-foot ladder should be 4 feet from the surface it's leaning against. Tom uses the L-shaped symbol stuck on each of the ladder's rails as his guide. If the L's short leg is horizontal and its long leg is plumb, the ladder is at the correct angle. Once a ladder is at the proper angle, it needs solid footing to stay that way. On soft ground, turn pivoting shoes so they dig in, or drive wooden stakes behind the shoes to prevent slippage. When the ground is too hard or too slippery or there's nowhere to drive stakes, tying off a lower rung to an immovable post or two is cheap insurance.

And never stand a ladder on a drop cloth or any other surface you can't depend on—such as the bed of a pickup truck. More than one person has been surprised by a ladder's lean after setting it up on frozen soil that turned soft—and unsupportive—as the day warmed.

It's tempting to load a ladder with accessories, but every one adds weight that you'll have to lug around. Some add-ons protect walls and gutters; others, such as self-leveling feet, improve safety. But common sense is more valuable than extras. Dee has seen people perched on the top rung of an extension ladder (you shouldn't go higher than the fourth rung from the top) or standing on one foot doing an aerial arabesque as they lean to one side ("Reach with your arms, not your body," says Dee). He's even seen people carrying fully extended ladders...while tottering backward toward power lines. If you'd like to meet your ancestors sometime soon, that would work.

Padded standoffs prevent sharp-edged ladder rails from putting scratches on walls.

Steel roof hooks safely hold a ladder to a roof peak; a pair of hooked ladders can be fitted with brackets to hold planks. This pair swings for storage.

Rubber booties that cover the top end of each ladder rail offer another way to protect walls from dents and scratches.

A sturdy welded-aluminum step makes long stays aloft more comfortable for over-worked feet. Hinged versions can pivot out of the way.

OR A LIFE. NEVER CLIMB HIGHER THAN 2 FEET BELOW THE TOP OF THE LADDER, AND DON'T SIT ON ITS TOP—YOUR WEIGHT CAN EASILY EXERT ENOUGH LEVERAGE TO TIP THE LADDER. DON'T CLIMB A CLOSED STEPLADDER, EITHER, EVEN IF IT SEEMS TO BE RESTING SECURELY AGAINST A WALL; IF IT'S ANGLED STEEPLY ENOUGH TO KEEP YOU FROM TIPPING BACKWARD, IT'S ANGLED ENOUGH FOR THE FEET TO SLIP OUT FROM UNDER YOU.

SOME STEPLADDERS HAVE STEPS ON BOTH SETS OF RAILS; THEY'RE THE ONLY MODELS THAT CAN BE USED FROM EITHER SIDE. IF YOU CLIMB OTHER STEPLADDERS FROM THE WRONG SIDE, THEY'LL MOST LIKELY BE RUINED. LIKE ANY TOOL, A LADDER NEEDS CARE. LIGHTLY LUBRICATE MOVING PARTS SUCH AS SPREADER BARS AND PULLEYS, AND CLEAN OFF SPILLED PAINT OR OIL RIGHT AWAY. SUNLIGHT EVENTUALLY DEGRADES A FIBERGLASS LADDER, EXPOSING FIBERS AND LETTING IN MOISTURE; SPOT-COVER THESE AREAS WITH POLYURETHANE PAINT. NEVER PAINT A WOOD LADDER, THOUGH, OR YOU'LL FIND IT TOO SLIPPERY TO STAY ON.

EXTENSION LADDERS RULE FOR OUTDOOR HEIGHTS, BUT THE STEPLADDER IS KING OF LOWER REACHES. MADE OF THE SAME MATERIALS AS EXTENSION LADDERS AND TO THE SAME LOAD RATINGS, STEPLADDERS ARE LIGHTWEIGHT AND MANEUVERABLE. BUT DON'T LET THE LOWER HEIGHT LULL YOU INTO CARELESSNESS, BECAUSE A FALL FROM EVEN A FEW FEET CAN RUIN A DAY—

safe steps

Self-leveling feet compensate for uneven terrain, so the rungs remain horizontal. This is particularly helpful when working near steps.

Two-toed feet keep an extension ladder from pitching over backward as it's being raised. Rubber caps improve skid resistance.

A stabilizer bar avoids windows and provides a temporary parking place for paint cans. Even better, it improves the ladder's stability.

This standoff rests on the roof, sparing gutters from metal-bending collisions and reducing the tendency of a ladder to slip sideways.

[**levels**]

SOMEWHERE OUT IN THE SPACE DIRECTLY IN front of master carpenter Norm Abram hangs a perfect horizontal line. The line is imaginary, but Norm wants to find it anyway because he's putting up a cabinet on the wall of a new kitchen and doesn't want the dishes to go sliding. "Of course, I'll never find a true level line," he says. "I'm going to be very close, but even my 48-inch level, over 50 feet, will be off half an inch or so." Or maybe more.

Most 48-inch spirit levels can be off by 1½ inches over 100 feet and still indicate a level plane. "Levels are limited by length," Norm says. "If you're leveling nice and straight 12-foot deck joists, even a 28-inch level will do. But if you're setting grade for a 90-foot foundation wall, you need a transit." Though leveling is what gave the tool its name, it can also plumb—find a perfectly vertical line. In fact, Norm uses his level mostly for this

purpose, because a wall is rarely more than 10 feet high, well within the working tolerances of the tool; a floor is much larger.

The accuracy of a level is relative, however. Many levels use 45-arc-minute vials, which are surprisingly insensitive to minor changes in pitch. (The arc-minute measurement relates to the number of degrees in a circle: There are 360 degrees in a circle and 60 arc minutes in each degree, so 45 arc minutes is three-quarters of a degree.) In a 45-arc-minute vial, the bubble won't move unless the level is tilted at least three-quarters of a degree. The smaller the arc-minute number, the greater the level's sensitivity. Look for a level that has at least a 35-arc-minute rating.

Vials are injection-molded out of acrylic or milled from a block of solid acrylic or made of Pyrex. The glass vials are often favored for being more consistent—they tend to expand and contract less with variations in temperature. Pyrex and acrylic vials are first filled with methanol, then welded shut with heat or ultrasound, though one manufacturer still caps glass vials with solder—the old-fashioned way.

Norm uses his level to locate studs when installing wallboard (above). After marking the floor or ceiling to identify the center of each stud, he puts up the wallboard, then uses the level and a pencil to make corresponding lines on the board.

When reading a level, always eyeball the vial straight on or you won't get accurate results. If a level has two pairs of marker lines on some vials (instead of one pair, as shown here), use the inner lines for leveling purposes. The outer lines are used for checking the slope of a pipe or a surface to ensure proper drainage.

[levels]

Norm steers clear of levels with adjustable vials, as they seem to get out of whack more easily than others; he prefers vials that are an integral part of the level. And as far as he's concerned, one level is just not enough. His everyday collection includes a 48-inch model for framing, a 28-inch model for checking door and window headers and an 18-incher for tight spaces. Sometimes he'll also use a water level, which takes advantage of the age-old knowledge that water seeks its own level. The device is simple: a sealed, flexible tube connected to a portable reservoir of water. To hang shelves, hang the reservoir on a nail and establish the level of water in the tube at the height you want to repeat; then move the tube anywhere in the room, wait for the water to settle and mark a level line.

* * *

SPECIALTY LEVELS

ON THE LOW END OF THE TECHNOLOGY SPECTRUM IS THE MODEST string level. It's a stubby thing, inexpensive and barely 4 inches long. Designed to hook, slothlike, onto a stretched string, they're among the least accurate of all levels but they're invaluable for quick level checks over long distances.

Used by masons to level brick and stone walls, string levels are also handy for leveling chalk lines before snapping them or for gauging the depth of a trench (by leveling a string between two stakes and measuring from string to trench bottom). But string levels can't be used to find plumb lines.

A mirror transit works like a surveyor's transit but is much easier to use. The operator sights a target within the rectangle on the measuring stick and sees a split image like that found in a camera viewfinder. When the target is raised or lowered to level, the split images come together. The unit, which operates by way of a mirror system, does not have to be leveled to make sightings.

Some levels, such as the laser/vial, attempt to blend new technology with old. A laser built into a spirit level effectively extends its length. Laser levels also tend to have much more accurate bubble vials—down to 5 arc minutes.

A laser perimeter level (also called a laser

« The accuracy of a level is relative. Many use 45-arc-minute vials, which are surprisingly insensitive to minor changes in pitch. »

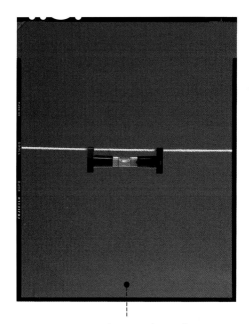

STRING LEVEL: Inexpensive and small enough to live in a shirt pocket, a string level is little more than a leveling vial with hooks. To improve accuracy, always make sure the level is equidistant from the string's supports.

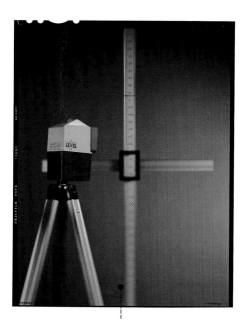

MIRROR TRANSIT: It's all done with mirrors. The simple sighting mechanism is helpful for laying foundations, checking the height of masonry walls, establishing drainage patterns and leveling large areas.

LASER/VIAL: When the laser is activated, a small red dot appears on walls as far as 400 feet away. This model is accurate to within $\frac{1}{4}$ inch at 60 feet. Leveling tasks requiring less precision can be handled by reading the leveling vials instead.

LASER PERIMETER: The turret of this tool projects the laser; it spins rapidly to streak walls with what looks like a continuous line. Never look directly at the laser itself, however—it can cause eye damage. The same holds true for any laser level.

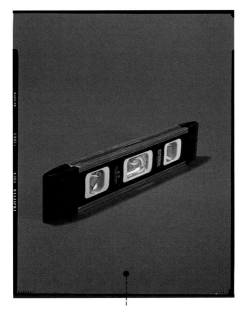

TORPEDO: The ideal level to keep in a toolbox or tuck into a tool belt, a torpedo (named for its tapered ends) is compact and inexpensive. It's light enough to rest atop anything.

SOUND AND LASER: Not only can you project a level laser line over great distances with this tool, but you can also "hear" level without having to stare at a vial. That's helpful in dim light or when you can't position yourself to see a leveling vial.

[levels]

beacon) creates a continuous line of light vertically or horizontally, and it can be hung from a wall bracket to create a level line around the top of a room—for example, to mark the perimeter of a dropped ceiling. Or it can be placed in a floor bracket to mark a level baseboard line or a plumb line on a wall, and it can also be mounted on a tripod to mark the room for chair rail. Another laser level (not shown) is the size of a tape measure but simultaneously projects two beams at 90 degrees to each other. Just set the tool down, and the pendulum-hung laser, held plumb by gravity, projects a pair of bright ruby-red dots on wall and ceiling surfaces, a real help when installing cabinets and molding. Flip the case

on its side, and the beams remain exactly 90 degrees apart, useful for tiling floors or laying out foundations. As with any laser level, beams can be difficult to see in bright sunlight.

The sleek torpedo level offers the quickest way to find plumb and level surfaces. Used by plumbers, electricians and home owners, torpedoes are tapered to make them easy to shove into a pocket. They are usually 9 inches long and can be magnetic (to stick to a pipe or a circuit-breaker box) or nonmagnetic. They're just the ticket for leveling a washing machine or hanging a picture.

Another approach adds sound to laser projection in an 18-inch level. The unit beeps continuously when level, making work easier in confined spaces, where bubble vials are difficult to see. A display panel shows the direction to move the unit to find level. A push of the slope button memorizes any angle so that it can be repeated, a trick useful for establishing pitches of roofs, decks and driveways. Accuracy is claimed to be within 3/8 inch at 50 feet.

Levels don't last forever, particularly when they hang around a hard-knocks job site. Don't put up with a damaged level—get rid of it. Norm has gone through at least seven 48-inch levels in the last 20 years. But when you buy one, don't assume that it's accurate just because it's new: Check it before you reach for your wallet. Place the level on a flat surface; then level the level by adding sheets of paper or thin shims under one end until a vial reads level. Carefully mark where the ends rest, then rotate the level end-for-end. If the vials still read level, it's a keeper.

C hecking For Proper Drainage: To encourage water to drain off the step (and away from the house), Norm wants each step to tilt slightly forward. If he's using a level that has only one pair of marker lines on each vial, he can eyeball the slope. With two pairs of lines, however, he could tilt the level until the bubble just touched an outer line; that would correspond to a slope of 1/4 inch per foot, perfect for drainage.

TECHNIQUES

L eveling A Step: Outdoor steps such as these granite blocks (above) must be level lengthwise. To reduce the possibility that slight irregularities in the stone's surface will throw his measurements off, Norm rests his level on a long, straight board; its extra reach bridges slight inconsistencies.

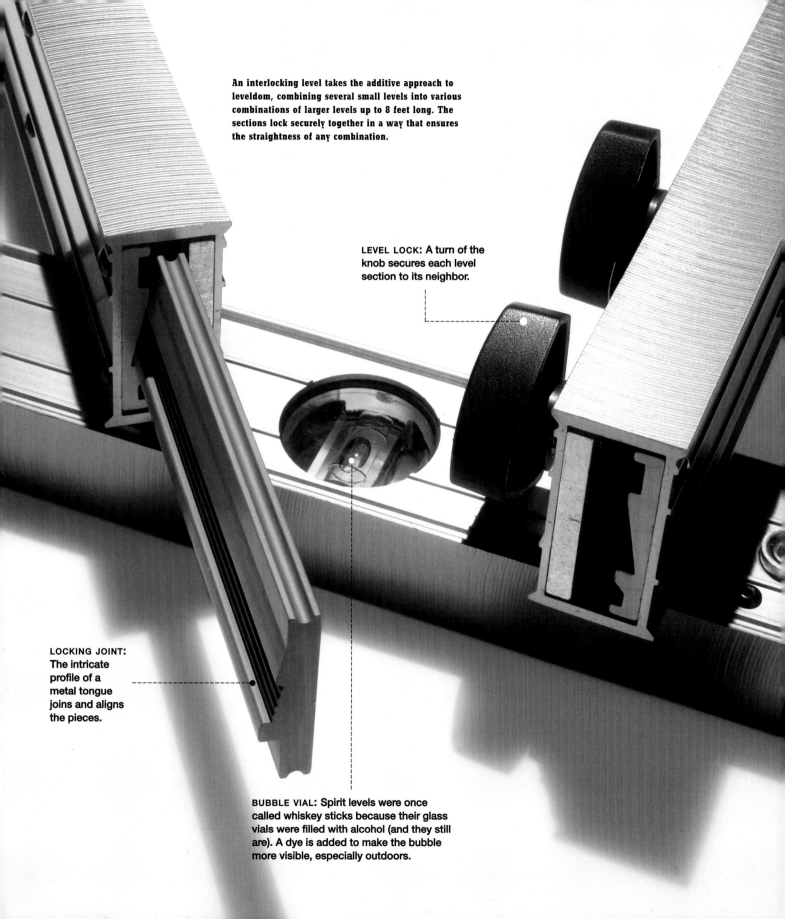

An interlocking level takes the additive approach to leveldom, combining several small levels into various combinations of larger levels up to 8 feet long. The sections lock securely together in a way that ensures the straightness of any combination.

LEVEL LOCK: A turn of the knob secures each level section to its neighbor.

LOCKING JOINT: The intricate profile of a metal tongue joins and aligns the pieces.

BUBBLE VIAL: Spirit levels were once called whiskey sticks because their glass vials were filled with alcohol (and they still are). A dye is added to make the bubble more visible, especially outdoors.

[**mechanicalscrewdrivers**]

A CENTURY AGO, WHEN MECHANICAL SCREWDRIVERS were still new, one factory owner hailed them as the "most glorious boon to the woodworker and mechanic since the invention of the lever." That seems like excessive praise, but anyone who's spent a few 10-hour days turning screws the old-fashioned way knows it's more tedious than milking a cow—and murder on the forearms. Some versions, like the Yankee, drive screws with a push; some ratchet with a twist; but all are a vast improvement over a standard screwdriver. With the right bit, they can drive nearly any kind of screw.

Bits to drive nearly any screw, including slotted, Phillips, Torx and those below, are available for mechanical screwdrivers.

Twelve-point

Triple Y

Spanner security

T-star

Quadrex

Octo-drive

T-cross

Allen

Robertson

Butterfly

A Yankee makes driving screws enormously easier. One or two pushes quickly spin the screw down into its pilot hole (made earlier by the same tool with a drill bit in the chuck). The basic design has remained the same for more than 70 years: An internal spring-loaded shaft twirls on threads cut in a crisscross spiral pattern. Moving a button on the handle reverses the direction of spin. One turn of the knurled brass collar locks the shaft in place, either at full extension or closed. From its closed position, the shaft can shoot out of its handle, making the sound of an angry rattlesnake. And it's nearly as dangerous if the bit is pointed at anyone. Play with a "loaded" Yankee and you can break a window with a launched bit. Ratcheting screwdrivers, on the other hand, pose no such danger, and they fit into a tighter space than a Yankee will, but

Mechanical screwdrivers, whether the push type or the ratcheting type, connect craftsmen to their work better than any power tool can. This spiral-threaded push driver was patented in 1897. It has a clockwise-threaded steel shaft inside a brass shaft spiraling counterclockwise. The user can engage either shaft by twisting its brass collar.

[mechanicalscrewdrivers]

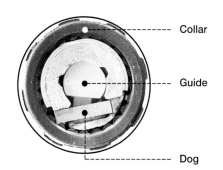

in 1923,
*North Brothers
of Philadelphia made
the first Yankee
screwdriver.
Stanley Tool Works,
which bought
the design 22 years
later, continues to
produce it.*

their tiny clicking dogs can't spin a screwhead as quickly. Still, they enable the hand to keep a firm grip and apply steady pressure as the screw turns, eliminating the frustration of slipping bits and the fatigue of excessive twisting. Ratcheting mechanisms are rated to withstand at least 220 inch-pounds of torque, much more than the 65 to 105 inch-pounds that humans can apply to a straight-handled screwdriver. In those tools with angled handles, the mechanisms have to withstand an extra 100 inch-pounds of torque for every inch the handle projects past the shaft's centerline.

What else can these mechanical marvels do besides drive screws? Look hard enough and you'll find such fittings as chuck adapters, push bits, hex sockets, pipe reamers and countersinks. The push bits alone will change your life. Never again will you drag out a drill, even a cordless one, just to pop a few pilot holes in the woodwork for curtain brackets.

Of course, many screws these days are driven with cordless drills. With one of these whining electric pistols, shooting screws requires only a trigger finger and a fully charged power cell; a robot can be programmed to do it. And that's the flip side of a power-driven fastener: Gone is the tactile connection between the worker, the wood and the wood screw, a subtle affinity of tool to hand that stops threads from stripping or heads from being mangled beyond redemption. Old-timers call it mechanic's feel. It used to be at the heart of all craft, but most craftsmen have adopted the cordless drill for its speed and efficiency. A mechanical screwdriver has other gifts, however. Unhurried and almost silent, it makes a soft *clickety-whir* and drives each screw a little differently. These are elegant and peaceful moments. Time is not always of the essence when the essence itself is timeless.

Collar

Guide

Dog

inside a ratchet

THE MECHANISM OF A TWIST-RATCHET SCREWDRIVER TAKES ONE OF TWO FORMS. SOME ROTATE THEIR SHAFTS WITH A SMALL CLICKING DOG-AND-SLOT DEVICE (LEFT); OTHERS USE A SILENT NEEDLE-BEARING MECHANISM. IN THE FORMER, A SPRING-LOADED METAL BAR (THE DOG) POPS INTO SLOTS AROUND THE INSIDE OF A METAL COLLAR. THE ANGLED DOG LETS THE COLLAR TURN IN ONE DIRECTION ONLY. WHEN THE GUIDE SLIDES THE DOG OVER, ROTATION REVERSES. IN CONTRAST, THE NEEDLE-BEARING RATCHET RELIES ON THE FRICTION OF A JAGGED OFF-CENTER WHEEL GRABBING A SMOOTH METAL HUB. A PLASTIC NEEDLE ANGLES THE WHEEL, DETERMINING THE DIRECTION IN WHICH IT HOLDS FAST.

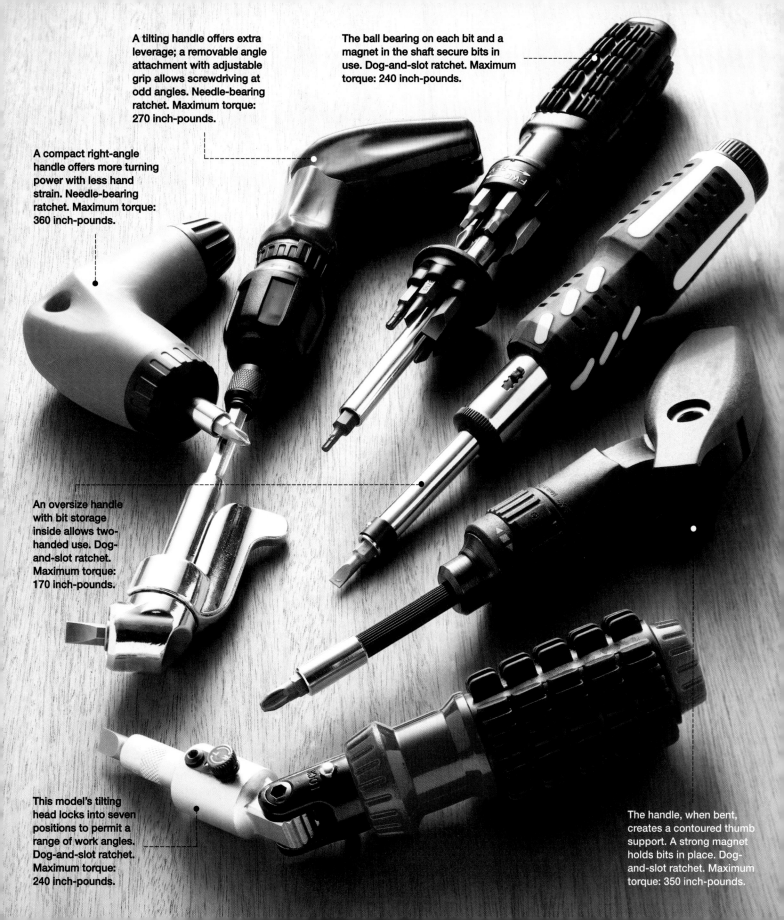

A tilting handle offers extra leverage; a removable angle attachment with adjustable grip allows screwdriving at odd angles. Needle-bearing ratchet. Maximum torque: 270 inch-pounds.

The ball bearing on each bit and a magnet in the shaft secure bits in use. Dog-and-slot ratchet. Maximum torque: 240 inch-pounds.

A compact right-angle handle offers more turning power with less hand strain. Needle-bearing ratchet. Maximum torque: 360 inch-pounds.

An oversize handle with bit storage inside allows two-handed use. Dog-and-slot ratchet. Maximum torque: 170 inch-pounds.

This model's tilting head locks into seven positions to permit a range of work angles. Dog-and-slot ratchet. Maximum torque: 240 inch-pounds.

The handle, when bent, creates a contoured thumb support. A strong magnet holds bits in place. Dog-and-slot ratchet. Maximum torque: 350 inch-pounds.

[**multi-tools**]

MULTIBLADE KNIVES were just the beginning: Now there's a family of can-do tools that cut, grip, twist and slice. Dubbed multi-tools for their ability to tackle any mission, these stainless-steel pocket toolboxes are mean-looking but ingenious. They're no substitute for bigger tools. . . except when none of those is at hand. *This Old House* host Steve Thomas carries one with a tough nylon-holstered plier/wire cutter (center right), miniature tools (screwdriver blades, knives, files) and convenience items (can and bottle openers) built into the handles. "I use it a lot when I'm sailing," he says.

Norm Abram takes a somewhat different approach to multi-tools. "In the shop," he says, "the right tool is always at hand." Still, he's not entirely oblivious to the convenience packed inside these gems of tool packaging. His favorite (near right) is a sturdy multi-tool with compound-leverage pliers: "When I helped assemble a neighbor's bird feeder," he

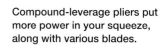

Compound-leverage pliers put more power in your squeeze, along with various blades.

The Novelty of locking-jaw pliers nearly overshadows a convenient thumb stud that makes the knife blade accessible.

Eleven Blades perform 23 functions, including those of a combination metal file and a hacksaw. Pliers complete the selection.

Sleek But Hefty, this 12-ounce heavyweight fits in surprisingly few blades. Its two fittings, however, accommodate extra screwdriver bits.

For electrical repairs, a wire stripper, crimper and needle-nose pliers are great.

This package of 13 tools opens easily with one hand.

« These stainless-steel pocket toolboxes are mean-looking but ingenious. »

admits, "it made me look good." Whether you're shinnied up a tree or headed to Fargo on a bike, a pocketful of multi-tool can solve almost any problem you're likely to encounter. Stash one in a tackle box, glove compartment, backpack—wherever light weight and versatility are crucial. Just be careful unfolding all those razor-sharp knife blades, even on models with blade locks.

A high-quality multi-tool costs more than a cheap pair of pliers, but plenty of models are available. You should be able to find the right one to suit whatever need you have.

A 6-Ounce Minimalist slims down to eight blades and is relatively lightweight, but that all comes at the expense of a safety lock.

Each Blade Can Fold Out whether pliers are open or folded; laminated jaws, rivet-pivot hinges and ergonomic grips allow for smooth handling.

Shedding Pliers saves so much weight and bulk on this multi-tool that scissors and a flashlight can snuggle in effortlessly.

[nailpullers]

THE ACT OF DRIVING NAILS IS OFTEN SET TO THE music of profanity—from bloody howls of unleashed eloquence, when the hammer accidentally drives a thumb, to a muttered syllable when the nail bends. But if the nail is perfectly driven and set flush for all eternity in the wrong spot, mere words will not suffice or remedy. Reversing such blunders requires a special tool, of which there are many. One of these, however, is not the carpenter's hammer. Though numerous nailectomies are performed with the claws of a hammer (or even with a pair of pliers), the tool doesn't work nearly as well as a tool with real pull.

The hallmark of a hammer, the bifurcated peen, was invented by the Romans. *Erratum maximum*: Immediately afterward, Rome fell. Yet somehow the shape of the hammer's claw seems ideal for pulling nails, and it's already in your hand so it's faster than hunting around for a more suitable tool. Carpenters have even put the fork of the hammer claw on a buried nail and then struck the face with another hammer. (The eye patch became popular at about the same time as this foolish trick.) One consequence of pulling nails with a hammer is broken hammer handles. That's why the perfect nail-pulling tool is the cat's-paw, an unbreakable steel bar with a spoon-shaped claw forged into at least one end.

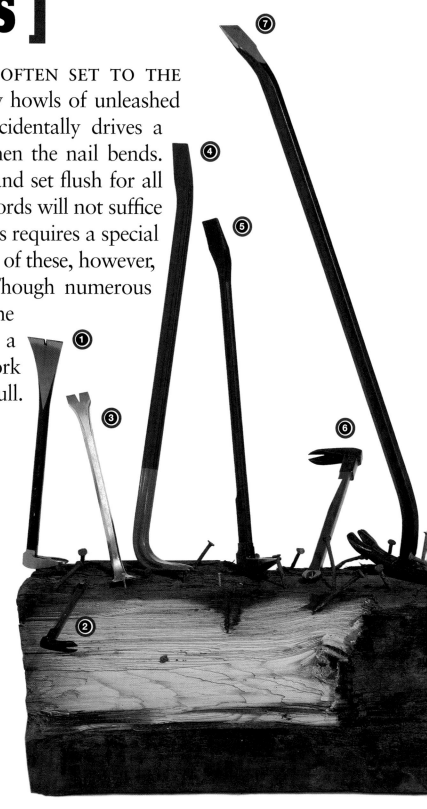

Japanese Nail Pullers (1, 2, 5, 6) have a pronounced L-shaped head with a flattened hammer-strike surface. The extra length of the head pulls nails out straighter than the traditional pawlike curve. Narrower claws make these tools right for removing finish and ring-shank nails.

Wrecking Bars (4, 7, 9), which range from 24 to 48 inches long, will rip out even the most stubborn 20d spikes. Their bent or curved chisel tails can separate boards that seem inseparable.

Flat Pry Bars (8) will remove nails, pull apart boards, raise doors or drywall sheets off the floor for hanging or level base cabinets. On salvage jobs, carpenters with pry bars in each hand can loosen anything—siding, flooring—at high speed and with little damage. They're indestructible.

The Common Two-Claw Cat's-Paw (10) lacks the leverage of its longer cousins but is a nail ferret extraordinaire and fits nicely into a tool belt.

Ram Pullers (11) have parrot-beaked pincers, which are driven under the nail head with the hammering force of the sliding cast-iron handle. The handle extends to increase leverage, and the curved foot keeps the pull straight. Ram pullers are perfect for pulling nails when you want to minimize damage to the wood.

A U-shaped Bracket (12) replaces the tail claw on this cat's-paw, making it useful for twisting joists perpendicular. It looks ridiculous but works like a charm.

Ripping Chisels (3, 13) are nightstick lengths of steel stock...and powerful persuaders. Some have a teardrop nail-pulling slot in the tail. They're at their best lifting lids on wooden crates.

Modern cat's-paws have two sets of claws, one each at the head and tail. The typical buried framing nail can be coaxed up with the curled kitty-paw-shaped head claw, but a nail driven deeply into awkward places requires the tail, which can zero in on the most inaccessible nail heads. If nails resist withdrawal, as galvanized ones invariably do, they can be yanked out the rest of the way with a flat bar or a crowbar or even tweaked out with nippers.

Norm Abram first used a cat's-paw when he was 15, working with his father. It's not a tool that got picked up often. "But when you needed it, it was there," Norm says. To extract nails with heads on or just above the surface of the wood, he places the paw's tips flat on the wood near the nail head. He then taps the back of the paw with a hammer to snag the nail shank in the paw's notch. When he rocks the handle back, the nail is history. Buried nail heads are a different matter and must be dug out. Norm holds the cat's-paw tips a quarter inch or so away from the nailhead, angling them about 45 degrees to the surface of the wood. As he hammers the tips into the wood, they snuggle in neatly just beneath the nail head; that's when he leans on the paw's handle to scoop out the nail cleanly. When it comes down to Norm versus a nail, there's only one possible outcome.

[**paintbrushes**]

STUCK HANDLE-DOWN into the back pocket of painter Pat Chism's white trousers, his favorite China-bristle paintbrush is ready for the first strokes of the day. Chism pulls it out with a swashbuckling motion and runs his fingers idly through the soft tips of the long black bristles. Despite several months of almost daily use in oil-based paints, the brush looks clean enough for him to lather up for a shave with it. He dips the brush halfway into a pot of viscous semigloss, then lays on and "tips off" a coat onto a door; primed wood disappears quickly beneath a glassy lake free of brush marks.

Minutes later, the same brush nudges a perfect line of paint along a molding's edge. Chism has the usual complement of modern painting tools (including spray gear) but in tight spots, when cutting in along walls and ceilings or finishing surfaces like cabinets and trim, he relies on that most ancient of tools: a brush.

Brushwork is efficient. It doesn't require enshrouding a room Christo style, in drop cloths and plastic film. Cleanup is faster. Control—with a little practice—can be as precise as calligraphy. And without the cacophony of rattling compressors, hissing nozzles and crackling rollers, a brush lets a painter work in tranquillity. But painting with a poorly made brush is more slapstick than Zen-like, so painters learn early to separate the good from the bad. The unmistakable feel of a good brush is like that of any other fine tool—you recognize it as soon as you pick it up. And you pay for it: Do-it-yourselfers accustomed to buying what pros call throw-aways are often aghast at the cost of fine handmade brushes, not realizing that they can last for decades if properly cleaned and stored.

The best ones have bristles packed, glued and bound to handles so securely that it's easier to pull a hair from your head than pluck one from the brush. But a cheap paintbrush, says painter John Dee, "sheds like a dog." It's

SYNTHETIC FILAMENTS: Equally at home in oil-based or latex paint, as long as the same brush isn't dipped in both.

HUMAN HAIR: Too limp to make a decent brush.

NYLON-POLY: Exploded tips simulate natural flagging.

OX HAIR: Soft, naturally flagged tips smooth wet paint.

This "pounder," so nicknamed because its abundant bristles can hold a pound of paint, once helped workers on bridges and ships stab thick paint into seams and crevices. Faux finishers now use it to stipple rough surfaces. When loading any brush, keep paint away from the ferrule, or the dried flecks that collect there will end up on the finish.

[paintbrushes]

OX HOCKEY: Extremely soft, ruddy hair from the ears of the South American and Asian ox is blended with bristle for body. Hockey-style handle reaches high as it maintains proper brush angle to wall.

BADGER BLENDER: Men who brush on shaving lather know the softness of badger. Faux finishers cherish its ability to blend and soften color. These fine 3-inch hairs come from Asia.

BOAR-BRISTLE OVAL: White *setola* (triple-bleached Italian boar) bristle fills the ferrule of this Italian-made housepainting and varnishing brush. Call them hogs, boars or swine, but their hair—and only their hair—can be called bristle.

Synthetic filaments have their place, but natural bristle and animal hair from around the world are prized for many more brush uses, from housepainting to decorative faux-finish work. How bristles and hair are processed—sorted, boiled, cleaned and mixed—remains a closely guarded secret.

PIG-BRISTLE SASH: Unlike the flat, angled sash brush typically found in the United States, this European sash-and-trim brush is round in cross section and has *setola* bristles, set in rubber, that taper like a pencil tip. It's perfect for painting the thin muntins on doors and windows. Old-time brush makers can distinguish between China bristle from pigs of wintry Qingdao (long and soft) and that of Chongqing, where the hogs wear short, stiff, summer-weight suits.

SQUIRREL SWORD STRIPER: A short, flat handle, easily turned with fingertips, guides European blue squirrel-tail hair gripped in a copper ferrule. The limpest of all brush hair, it drags a perfect line for painting automobile pinstripes and signs.

HORSEHAIR STUCCO: An old-fashioned house-painter's brush has a pecan beaver-tail handle and a leather-bound finger-cushioning ferrule. This style blends bristle with 30 percent horsehair. Coarse, brittle and nonflagging, horsehair was an adulterant used by unscrupulous brush makers during the bristle shortages of World War II.

[paintbrushes]

also hard to control, can't cut a clean line or get paint to level and has a tendency to drip when going between can and surface. "They can be uncomfortable—poorly balanced—and just won't hold up to cleaning."

When the pros look for a good brush, the process is often more tactile than visual. Standing at a rack full of new brushes, they remove the stiff keeper protecting the bristles and make a close inspection. The business end gets a firm tug to see how well anchored the bristles are. Then they push, stroke and fan the brush against the back of a hand or a chin, feeling for the softness that indicates supple, extensively flagged tips (the brush equivalent of split ends). Like a legion of tiny feather dusters, these tips help smooth brush marks as well as push paint into a surface's microscopic crevices. Many painters believe a brush still does this better than

anything. Dee, for one, insists on brushing siding seconds after he spray-paints it in order to work in the finish.

The construction of a brush determines whether it carries paint to a wall for hours with dripless legerdemain or needs frequent stops for reloading. Most ferrules are not packed solid with hair or filament. Spread them and you'll see a spacer plug, which creates a reservoir that fills with paint as the brush is dipped in the can. As the brush is stroked across a surface, paint squeezes along tapered filaments to be dispersed by the flagged tips. The void also lets solvent penetrate into the ferrule area during cleaning. Brushes without spacers, such as the finest European brushes for oil-based paints, work just as well, say some; the extra bristles lift more paint from the can. Dee uses both kinds but says the solid-packed brushes are harder to clean.

A good brush is more than just bristles stuck on a stick.

Black China Bristle

Ferrule (stainless steel)

Spacer

Oval Heel

Beaver-Tail Handle

Epoxy
(for holding bristles)

cleaning a brush

BLOCK STIPPLER: Has unbleached China bristle; use with flat tapping motion to remove paint during faux-finishing work.

FLATTING BRUSH: A 6-inch width of bristles speeds wall and ceiling work.

FLOGGER: Also called a dragger: Simulates a wood-grain effect.

"MAN HELP": The round brush fits onto a long handle or pole.

OVAL HEEL: Shape improves the brush's paint-holding ability.

STENCIL BRUSH: Short bristles stand up to constant dabbing.

THOROUGH AND FREQUENT CLEANING—AND MATCHING THE BRUSH TO THE PROPER PAINT—ARE THE KEYS TO THIS LONG-LIVED TOOL. A PROFESSIONAL PAINTER WON'T HESITATE TO STOP FOR THE FEW MINUTES IT TAKES TO CLEAN A BRUSH THAT FEELS SATURATED AND UNRESPONSIVE OR THAT HAS PAINT DRYING IN THE FILAMENTS NEAR THE FERRULE. ANIMAL-HAIR BRUSHES ARE BEST USED IN OIL-BASED (ALKYD) FINISHES: WATER MAKES THEM TOO FLOPPY. NYLON AND POLYESTER BRUSHES CAN BE USED IN EITHER PAINT, BUT AVOID GOING BACK AND FORTH BETWEEN THE TWO WITH THE SAME BRUSH. "THERE ARE SOLVENTS IN LATEX PAINT THAT REACT WITH THE OILS IN ALKYDS AND LEAVE A GUMMY MESS IN THE FERRULE," SAYS DEE. "ONCE IT HAPPENS, THE BRUSH IS RUINED." DEE MARKS BRUSH HANDLES TO DISTINGUISH THEM: RED FOR OIL, BLUE FOR LATEX.

EVEN WITH THE BEST CARE, ANY BRUSH WILL FLAG OUT AND STIFFEN UP AFTER REPEATED WASHINGS. SURFACE FRICTION WEARS IT DOWN AS WELL. PAINTER PAT CHISM REACHES FOR JUST SUCH A STUBBY, RETIRED-FROM-PAINTING BRUSH TO FLICK DUST OFF THE TOP OF DOOR TRIM. "IT STARTED OFF PAINTING LIKE ANY OTHER," HE SAYS. "NOW IT'S MY DUSTER. THERE'S ALWAYS SOME LIFE LEFT IN A GOOD BRUSH."

How To Clean A Brush: 1. To revive a rock-hard brush, soak it overnight in water-rinsing brush cleaner; then wire-brush it against a flat surface. It won't paint like new, though. 2. A good, expensive brush deserves to be cleaned well and often. With oil paints, wear rubber gloves and vigorously force thinner into bristles. Tip brush up to get solvent well down into ferrule. 3. Rinse four times. Save thinner for reuse; solids will settle. After each rinse, spin dry; then straighten bristles and banish paint particles with a brush comb. 4. Wrap bristles in a keeper so they stay straight. Store flat or hang. (Brushes for some latex paints should be washed with soap and water, then in a water-rinsing solvent to rid the filaments of residue.)

[**paintscrapers**]

FOR SHEER PLEASURE in the work, no renovation job gives less than scraping. It builds character, not happiness. To appreciate how hours can flit by—like glacial epochs—try pulling paint off hand-carved woodwork covered in white lead paint by some Victorian vandal, followed down the decades by coats of salmon, lime, chartreuse and mauve. Afterward, for even more personal growth, strap on some kneepads and take to peeling the varnish off an oak floor. Scrape a few planks and you'll be having a swell time—just like that blistering August weekend when you insulated the attic.

Scrape may have an unpleasant onomatopoeic sound, but the alternatives are even uglier. Sanding by hand is too slow and dusty, power sanding erases details and leaves gouges, and chemical stripping creates a toxic goo that still requires scraping. Together, a well-honed scraper and a pure heart can lead to ecstasies of scraping perfection, those heavenly moments when each stroke peels away long strips of encrusted paint to reveal the lovely wood hidden beneath. Anyone still scraping with grandfather's heirloom, however, will find this job pluperfect hell.

Only one thing makes the use of an old scraper even tolerable: You have to keep the blades honed by filing them every five minutes. (Old paint is surprisingly abrasive and, often, toxic.) Use a file, and stroke it toward the edge of the blade but not off it, which leaves a fragile edge. After that, the work will go faster, and a week of scraping paint off the side of your house will age you only five years.

There is, however, a secret for easy scraping: using a variety of good modern tools, exceedingly sharp. Some should have wide blades that peel the crud off in a single sweeping pass; others should fit narrow planes and tiny crevices where the corner of a wide scraper would do more damage than good.

All paint scrapers are divided into two

« The pushers: Push scrapers work best when used against the wood, the corners will dig in and leave rippled are the natural choice for wood because they have smaller,

types: push and pull. The most common push scrapers look like double-wide putty knives with stiff blades designed to slip under and pop off loose paint. The best ones have full-tang blades that go from the working edge to the handle, which can range from fairly standard to cleverly ergonomic, and are made of rubber, nylon or wood. Some push scrapers have hammering surfaces on the butt; others have screw sockets for poles to lengthen the reach. These work well for flooring adhesive, putty and caulk softened with a heat gun or

for well-soaked wallpaper, but they tend to slide over all but the most thoroughly exfoliated surfaces or nose-dive into wood grain.

A pull scraper, on the other hand, can exert more downward thrust and sink the blade under the paint. The tool can go into the corners of tiny little reveals or scrape down bowling alleys with equal ease, and the blade can be switched to its sharper edge when it gets dull. Most modern pull scrapers have removable blades with two or more edges, in widths from 1 to 5 inches.

choosing a scraper

BLADES HELD AT AN ANGLE SLIGHTLY TOWARD THE HANDLE WON'T DAMAGE THE WOOD AS EASILY AS BLADES THAT ARE HELD PERPENDICULAR TO THE WOOD. ONE FAVORITE TYPE HAS TWO HANDLES AND EIGHT INTERCHANGEABLE STAINLESS-STEEL BLADES. THEY REQUIRE FREQUENT SHARPENING, BUT THEIR CURVACEOUS EDGES CAN SCOOP OUT THE MOST INTRICATE GROOVES, FLUTES AND OGEES FROM PAINT-SMOTHERED MOLDINGS.

THE LATEST IN PULL-SCRAPING TECHNOLOGY IS TUNGSTEN CARBIDE, A HARDER-THAN-ALMOST-ANYTHING ALLOY THAT SAVES A LOT OF BLADE FILING. THE ADS CLAIM THAT A CARBIDE BLADE IS TWO AND A HALF TIMES HARDER THAN THE BEST STEEL, AND THEY MAY BE RIGHT. OF COURSE, CARBIDE REPLACEMENT BLADES COST THRICE AS MUCH AS STEEL AND REQUIRE A DIAMOND-STUDDED HONING STONE TO TOUCH UP THEIR EDGES. BUT IN SCRAPING, MONEY SPENT IS SWEAT SAVED.

WHEN SHOPPING FOR SCRAPERS, TRUST YOUR HANDS. IF THE HANDLE IS SHAPED TO REDUCE FATIGUE, THE TOOL WILL SEEM LIKE AN EXTENSION OF YOUR ARM. LABELS SUCH AS "CONTRACTOR'S GRADE" AND "PROFESSIONAL QUALITY" SOUND NICE, BUT "FULL WARRANTY" IS MORE REASSURING. AND THEN THERE'S "GUARANTEED FOREVER." ISN'T THAT JUST ABOUT HOW LONG YOUR FIRST SCRAPING JOB SEEMED TO LAST?

with a heat gun or chemical stripper. If pressed too hard gouges on the surface. The pullers: Pull scrapers more stable blades, making it easier to apply pressure. »

[paintscrapers]

The beveled chisel edge of a 1½-inch scraper helps a blade slide under paint and curl it off.

Stiff, rust-resistant stainless-steel blades remove paint better than flexible blades, which are more suitable for puttying.

This scraper's bent shaft spares knuckles a scraping.

An ergonomically designed rubber-and-plastic handle includes a spot for thumb or forefinger to guide pushing pressure.

Standard razor blades remove errant paint strokes from glass. A spritz of water prevents scratching.

A wallpaper scraper strips most efficiently when angled at about 30 degrees. Its head unscrews to accept a longer handle for out-of-reach areas.

Interchangeable stainless-steel blades offer multiple profiles for scraping molding, trim and grooves.

Four-edged blades reduce the number of sharpening interruptions.

A three-edged scraper's perpendicular blade limits its angle of attack on paint but works wonders on glue cleanup, and the points reach into cracks and crevices.

Hand-friendly handles have a 20-degree blade angle that rips off paint without damaging wood. Both handles are fitted with blades of carbide, which keeps its edge 50 times longer than stainless steel. Designed for detail work, the 1-inch triangular blade rotates twice to prolong use.

Old-fashioned paint scrapers offer a wide wooden head for two-handed work.

[**pipeclamps**]

THE BACK OF TOM SILVA'S truck looks like a clamp warehouse. How many does he have back there? "Dozens. Hundreds. You know the old saying." Yep. Too many clamps are not enough. A million clamps is a good start. And variations on those. But when it comes to the big jobs, the ones that call for clamps with plenty of length and a strong bite, Tom reaches for his pipe clamps. "They're inexpensive, and I can use them a dozen different ways," Tom says, tightening a trio of 24-inch pipe clamps he's using to glue up stock for a kitchen project. Minutes earlier, he used some 12-inch pipe clamps to squeeze together the stiles on a cabinet assembly. Later in the day, he'll use several 9-foot clamps to hold square a custom-built door as he assembles it. Helpful as they are,

« You know the old saying. Yep. Too many

A pipe clamp is ingenuity at work, a deviously simple device up for nearly any clamping job. Some brands have a reversible head and a specially designed crank handle, so the clamp can double as a spreader—handy for straightening bowed studs, for example.

¾-Inch galvanized pipe

Tail stop

Sliding head

Steel screw

Handle

Stationary head

however, pipe clamps can ruin a project if they're used improperly. Tom always applies an equal amount of pressure with each clamp, and to keep from bowing a panel during glue-up, he alternates clamps top and bottom.

Pipe clamps have two major components: the clamp fixtures (consisting of a tail stop and a head assembly) and the pipe. The tail stop slides along the length of the pipe and contains a spring-loaded clutch mechanism that grabs the pipe at any point to prevent the stop from slipping once it has been set. On the head assembly, a screw with square threads (for greater strength and durability) applies steady pressure against the workpiece from the opposite direction. The tail stop is the part most likely to wear out, and replacement parts are sometimes available but the mechanism itself isn't worth replacing. It's easier and not much more expensive to pick up new clamp fixtures.

are not enough. A million clamps is a very good start. »

Fixtures are designed to fit ½- or ¾-inch pipe. Inexpensive black-steel pipe is preferred by some. The surface is less slippery than that of galvanized pipe, so the clutch mechanism can dig in. But most contractors, including Tom, find that galvanized pipe works just as well. Clamp fixtures and pipes can be purchased separately at hardware stores, home centers or through woodworking-tool catalogs.

One of the beauties of pipe clamps is that they're easy to extend. There's no need to haul around heavy, cumbersome lengths of pipe when it's possible to use a coupling—a pipe fitting with female threads at each end—to join two or more pipes for the reach needed to clamp together an entire run of cabinetry or

glue up a large piece of furniture. For a pipe to be extended, it must be threaded at both ends: one end to accept the head assembly and the other end for the coupling. Prethreaded pipe is readily available, but Tom prefers to shop at his favorite pipe store: whatever house he's demolishing. Pipe wrested from old heating and plumbing systems is free; all he has to do is spend a couple of bucks at a plumbing supply store to have the pipe threaded. But if you have pipe dies and plenty of extra time, you can thread pipes yourself.

Because the clamp fixtures are mounted on pipe instead of on a flat bar like similar clamps, the tail stop can be rotated to different positions. Tom finds this feature particularly

[pipeclamps]

helpful when he has to install intersecting runs of kitchen cabinets. After hooking the clamp's head over a face-frame stile on one cabinet, he slides the tail stop down the pipe and swivels it 90 degrees to catch a rail on the adjoining cabinet. Only light pressure is needed to draw the casework together and hold it steady until he can secure it permanently with screws.

But a whole rack of pipe clamps (or even a million) won't solve every clamping problem. You'll need others (below) before considering yourself ready for anything.

clamps for the memories

A PIPE CLAMP IS GREAT FOR BIG JOBS, BUT FORGET ABOUT USING A CLAMP TO SQUEEZE TOGETHER THE MITERED CORNERS OF A PICTURE FRAME OR THE BUILT-UP EDGE OF A SOLID-SURFACE COUNTERTOP. THERE ARE HUNDREDS OF DIFFERENT CLAMPS, EACH SUITED TO A DIFFERENT TYPE OF WORK, BUT MOST ARE VERSIONS OF THOSE SHOWN HERE. WHEN IT COMES TO BUYING CLAMPS, THERE ARE TWO RULES TO FOLLOW: ALWAYS BUY THEM IN PAIRS, AND GO FOR QUALITY—NOTHING IS WORSE THAN HAVING A CLAMP GIVE UP JUST WHEN YOU NEED IT THE MOST.

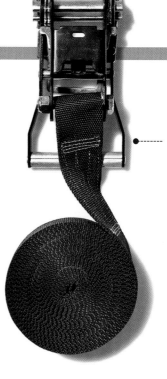

RATCHET-BAND CLAMP: This is the best clamp for securing several items or oddly shaped projects such as chair backs and segmented columns.

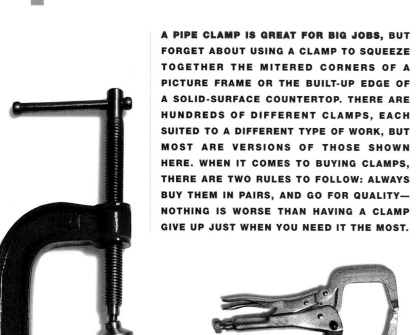

C-CLAMP: Versatile and useful in tight spaces, they range in size from 2 inches to more than a foot.

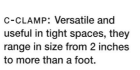

LOCKING-BAR CLAMP: Jaws can be set to a fixed clamping capacity, making these good for repetitious work. Pressure can be released with one hand simply by squeezing the release lever on the handle.

A Pipe That's Threaded at the ends can be extended with ease using a threaded coupling (left). To be extendable, a pipe must be threaded at both ends, one end to accept the head assembly and the other end for the coupling.

T om Is Careful not to overtighten pipe clamps (far left), as that would force too much glue out of the joints and dent the wood. Some clamps come with nonslip plastic pads that help to protect the wood, but Tom often uses spare bits of cardboard or scraps of wood, which he attaches to the jaws with double-stick tape to keep the pieces from dropping off at the last moment.

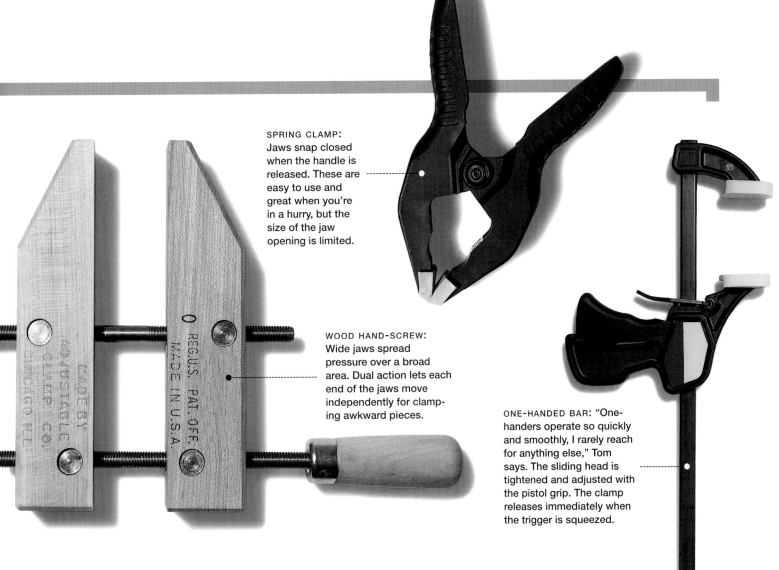

SPRING CLAMP: Jaws snap closed when the handle is released. These are easy to use and great when you're in a hurry, but the size of the jaw opening is limited.

WOOD HAND-SCREW: Wide jaws spread pressure over a broad area. Dual action lets each end of the jaws move independently for clamping awkward pieces.

ONE-HANDED BAR: "One-handers operate so quickly and smoothly, I rarely reach for anything else," Tom says. The sliding head is tightened and adjusted with the pistol grip. The clamp releases immediately when the trigger is squeezed.

[**pliers**]

IN A PINCH, YOU CAN'T BEAT A PAIR OF PLIERS. They replicate the tender grip of finger and thumb in hardened steel, amplifying muscles with the power of leverage. The offspring of blacksmiths' tongs, pliers have evolved into a family of shapes and sizes suited for dozens of specific tasks: fastening, pulling, twisting, squeezing, opening and cutting. With nose and jaw shapes tailored for grappling with particular objects, pliers poke into tight spots and reach around corners. No electrician, plumber or carpenter could get along without pliers, as tool chests at any job site can attest to.

to set

locking pliers, adjust the jaws so that they close on the object to be squeezed. Then open the jaws and twist the adjustment knob a quarter turn. Now the pliers will grip firmly yet release with ease.

Electrical contractor Paul J. Kennedy uses a pair of square-nosed, thick-jawed linesman's pliers to pop blanks out of electrical boxes, pull cable through walls, cut and strip wire, and twist and trim its ends for wire nuts. Whenever *This Old House* plumbing and heating contractor Richard Trethewey works under a sink, he reaches for a large pair of groove-joint pliers. He says the secret to using them is to bed the jaws against the fitting so that the pliers make contact with three sides, or else they'll round-over the fitting. Another trick he uses is to rotate these pliers toward the smaller, lower jaw, which tightens their grip thanks to a 45-degree bend at the knuckle. For picking small stuff out of narrow spots, Trethewey goes for needlenose pliers.

"If you drop a screw down into the valve seat, you'll be lost without them," he says. Norm Abram carries linesman's pliers, locking pliers and groove-joint pliers during demolition work, when he deals with live wires, frozen bolts and rusty pipes.

At their simplest, pliers consist of two crossed steel levers pivoting on a pin that joins them. Their mechanical advantage runs between 2 to 1 and 5 to 1, which translates into about 400 pounds of squeeze. Jaw power can be increased by moving the plied object closer to the pin, by shifting your grip outward on the handles or simply by getting a bigger pair of pliers. The pliers' pivot has been the focus of endless tinkering and ingenious metalworking. Bolts and rivets were the

« They replicate the tender grip of finger and thumb in hardened steel, amplifying muscles with the power of leverage. »

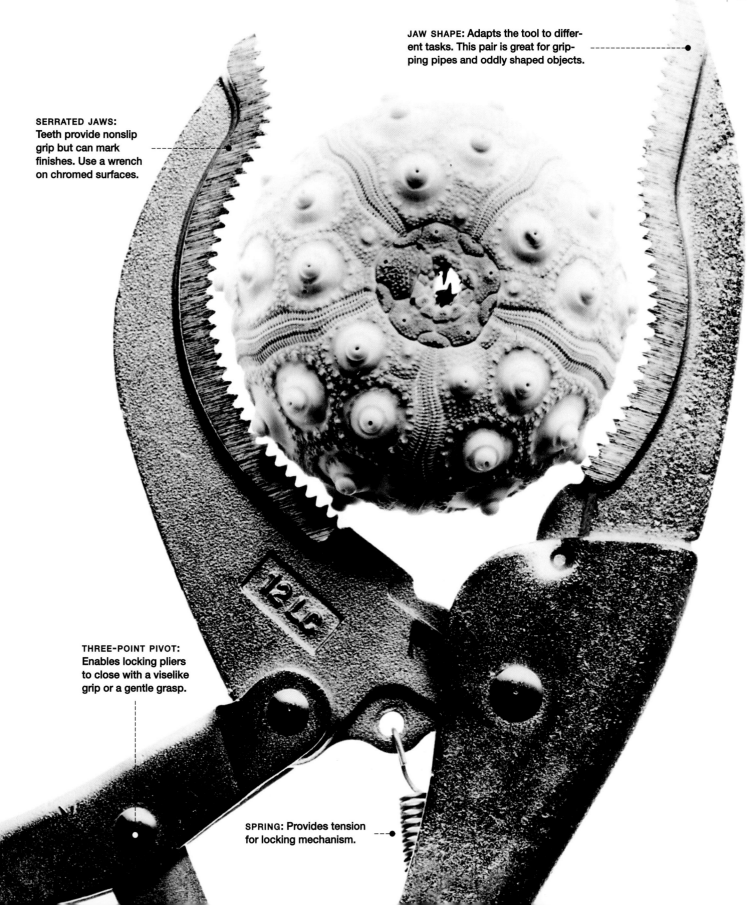

JAW SHAPE: Adapts the tool to different tasks. This pair is great for gripping pipes and oddly shaped objects.

SERRATED JAWS: Teeth provide nonslip grip but can mark finishes. Use a wrench on chromed surfaces.

THREE-POINT PIVOT: Enables locking pliers to close with a viselike grip or a gentle grasp.

SPRING: Provides tension for locking mechanism.

[pliers]

This pair of multiple slip-joint pliers has curved jaws for handling PVC pipe.

earliest pivots. But bolts work loose, and rivets get sloppy. The box joint, typical of linesman's and needlenose pliers, remains strong and tight for a lifetime but is difficult to make. The joint requires forging a cylindrical pivot on one arm, opening an eye of matching exactness in the other, fitting the two together hot, then reforging to a tight fit that still rotates. The best ones glide open and closed with the wobble-free smoothness of a bank-vault door. Not many smiths could fashion such a pivot, and even today manufacturers are secretive about the process. Box-joint pliers are fine for grabbing skinny wires, but anything thicker—a pipe or a nut—is beyond their grasp; the jaws just slip off. Jaws grip best when they are parallel, and the jaws on fixed-pivot pliers are parallel only when closed.

Early attempts to widen the range of bite led to slip-joint pliers, the ubiquitous knuckle-skinning tool with the figure-eight slot. A more successful solution appeared around 1920, when a Nebraska blacksmith named William Petersen tinkered his way to the compound-action, three-pivot pliers now known as locking pliers. Petersen's pliers self-lock, produce up to a ton of squeeze and have screw-adjustable jaws for optimal grip. After Petersen figured out how to stamp the handles from sheet steel —a faster, cheaper process than hand- or drop-forging—his triumph was complete. Today every tradesman carries at least one pair. The

tools are powerful enough to crimp-seal a spurting water line but somewhat cumbersome to adjust. Howard Manning, the chief engineer at Champion Tools, solved that problem in 1933 when he unhinged the pivot and created Channellocks. The drop-forged and machined jaws of Manning's pliers slip into as many as eight tongue-and-groove arcs, giving one tool a no-slip jaw range of more than 2 inches. Channellocks do have their drawbacks. Every time the jaws need repositioning, the two handles have to be opened wide enough for the grooves to disengage. Also, if the jaws aren't perfectly parallel, there's no way to fine-tune a drop-forged arc to correct the problem.

Enter William Warheit, who in 1987 invented the first self-adjusting pliers. His pliers, marketed as Robo Grips, have a cam-and-ratchet mechanism that automatically positions the pivot so the jaws remain parallel as the handles are squeezed. The tool is also simple to manufacture. Both the handles and the jaws of Robo Grips are stamped out of mild steel sheets, which are then hardened and riveted together around plastic inserts. Warheit's invention is a leap forward in pliers design, but it probably won't be the last one: Pliers evolution shows no signs of slowing. Every few years, a new version of Vise-Grips shows up, and now self-locking Robo Grips are sold alongside the originals. The quest for perfect pliers continues.

A Gallery Of Grippers: Needlenose pliers (at right, top row), with their hard-to-make, hard-to-break pivots and arced handles, come in a variety of shapes. 1. Bent needlenose pliers help speed work inside electrical chassis. 2. Stripping pliers remove wire insulation without cutting the wire beneath. 3. Retaining-ring pliers open when squeezed. 4. Grabbers pull insulated sleeves from spark plugs. 5. Cranked-nose pliers excel at prying. 6. Round-nosed ones bend thick copper wire into neat loops around the terminal screws on electrical outlets. Name A Job And You'll Find A Pair Of Pliers To Make It Easier: 7. These Swedish-made pliers have fast-opening jaws that adjust with a touch on a red button. 8. Fence tools are Wild West originals, created for cowpokes who needed one tool to cut and crimp barbed wire and also to pound and remove fence staples. 9. Heavyweight linesman-style pliers are favorites of ironworkers, who twist wire to tie one reinforcing bar to another; the dogleg at the end of one handle keeps their hands from slipping when they pull the wire tight.

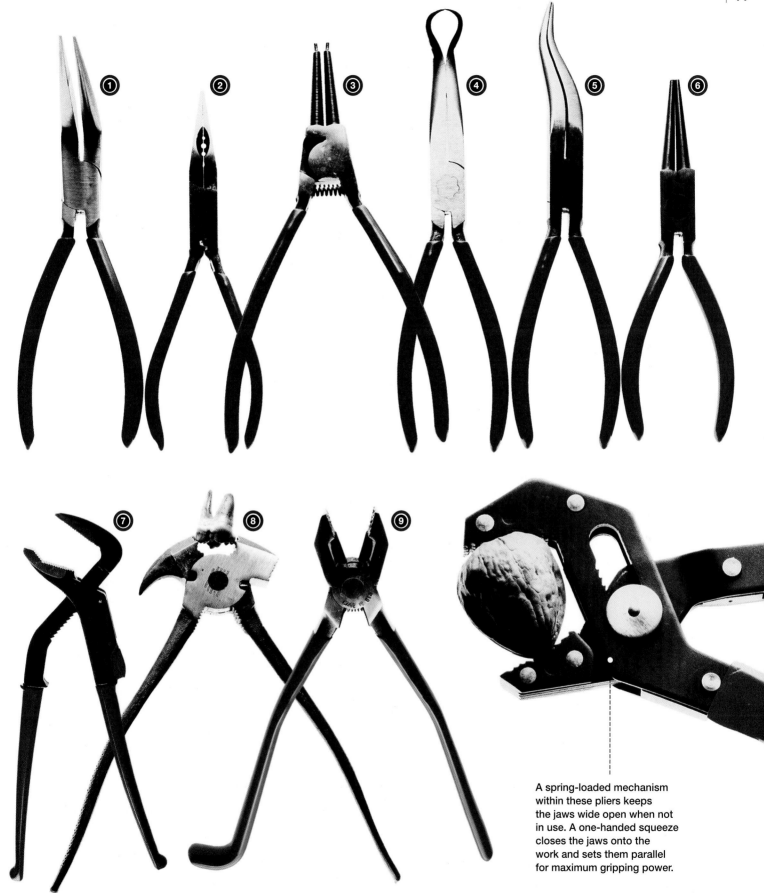

A spring-loaded mechanism within these pliers keeps the jaws wide open when not in use. A one-handed squeeze closes the jaws onto the work and sets them parallel for maximum gripping power.

[**plumbbobs**]

SO SIMPLE, SO ELEGANT, SO basic: A weight at the end of a string, a point at the end of the weight, and when the weight stops moving, that line is plumb, Bob. A plumb bob, powered by gravity, always points down to create a reliable vertical line for such jobs as plumbing walls, installing vent stacks and laying brick chimneys. Norm uses his most often for plumbing doorjambs. Sure, you can use a level to find a plumb line, but that tool works best when there's already some surface to rest it against. Plumb lines in space, however, are for plumb bobs to find. You can trust a tool named Bob.

Self-reeling plumb bobs simplify window and doorjamb installation. A spring-loaded pin holds the case on a wood jamb. Measuring the line's distance from the jamb at any point shows if the jamb is plumb.

Plumb bobs were already old when the Egyptians used them to determine meridian lines and orient the pyramids. Later, the Romans combined bobs with primitive transits called *groma* to build roads. Not surprisingly, inventors during the Industrial Revolution found ways to improve the design, especially for string storage. Many plumb bobs from that era have internal reels to take up the line or flanged bobbin caps or even swiveling bobbins. A magnificent diversity evolved, and you can find plumb bobs shaped like teardrops and turnips, bullets and balls, weighing anywhere from an ounce to 50 pounds. It's easy to see why some people collect them.

Even the squished-teardrop shape of a common chalk box lets it moonlight as a plumb bob—though with all the elegance of a rock. Somewhat better is a steel bob, blessed with a low cost that builders love. But just once hold a bob of brass in your hand,

and you'll never want another. Warm and smooth, gleaming like a sunrise or hand-worn and tarnished to the color of an old penny, a machined brass bob will last forever. Whatever the substance, a plumb bob should have a steel tip that can be unscrewed and replaced, because it takes all the grief if a dropped bob strikes a hard object.

Simple though it is, a plumb bob takes some practice to operate. Indoors, a tiny flattened bob works very well for papering walls, because wallpaper must begin with a perfectly vertical line. But if gravity is the plumb bob's best friend, wind is its nemesis. Outdoors, the longer the line, the heavier the bob must be to combat wind movement. However, the heavier the bob, the longer it must fight the inertia keeping it moving. One trick is to steady the point with two fingers, touching it gently now and then to keep it still.

Once the knotted end of the line has been captured beneath the plumb bob's knurled cap, the line will be centered above the tip.

the tiny hole *in the tip of a plumb bob? Slip a nail through the hole to serve as a handy lever as you unscrew a damaged tip.*

When the bob stops moving, mark the spot under the point. A house begins just this way, with a string of white nylon stretched from here to there between notched batter boards. The string forms a rectangle, the rectangle describes the foundation, and the foundation is committed to earth by a plumb bob.

The steel tip of this plumb bob can be unscrewed and replaced if damaged or worn. It's a good idea to keep a spare handy.

Plumb bobs without a replaceable tip often have blunter noses to improve their durability.

[rasps]

WHEN YOUR HAND CRAVES A WOODEN handle, soft to the touch and pleasing to the eye, there's a way to shape it to your heart's desire—with a rasp. Where this toothy hunk of metal meets wood, it cannot help but make pleasing arcs out of boring straight lines. Pull a cabinetmaker's rasp from its sheath and feel the heft as it pricks your palm with hundreds of sharp metal teeth. Like most woodworking rasps, this one has two abrading surfaces—rounded and flat—and tapers toward the tip (fusiform, for you Scrabble players). The metal tang fits snugly into a turned wood handle. Bear down on a board and round off its sharp edges; each stroke makes a hollow *zoof, zoof,* as fine shavings drift to the floor. Simple. Effective. Satisfying.

PLANING RASPS: The perforated sheet of steel held taut by a handle is covered either with tiny teeth or with bladelike edges.

Although they resemble files, their metalworking brethren, rasps feed exclusively on soft substances like wood, plaster and plastic, any of which would instantly clog a file's shallow ridges. The scores of sharp, pointed teeth on a rasp give it the same natural cutting action as a cat sculpting a cube of butter. No other tool can so quickly and efficiently remove and shape material with the same delicate touch.

Somewhere in the toolboxes of artisans who make custom doors, cabinets and furniture, you'll always find a rasp or three. Woodcarvers shape the petals and umbos of ornamental rosettes with tiny double-curved rifflers; perfectionist trim carpenters use the same rifflers to neatly excise the last bit of waste from a piece of coped crown molding. The 2-foot horse rasp—farriers use them to give a horse a pedicure—can magically erase big splinters and bulging knots on the walls of log houses. Bakers once had bread rasps to remove burnt crust or cinders on the bottoms of loaves. But in the hands of a master woodworker such as furniture-maker Sam Maloof, a rasp becomes a magic wand, revealing airy curves hidden inside homely blocks of wood.

Rasps may appear indestructible, but after making piles of sawdust, their teeth get dull. If left in a toolbox to bang against other tools, they wear out even faster. A dull rasp is no fun to use and can't be resharpened, so store rasps in individual canvas or leather sheaths. When one finally dies, recycle it via a local blacksmith who might make a knife out of it.

A belt sander would be faster, no doubt, at turning hard edges into sensuous contours, and a router would bring uniformity to the task. But a rasp lets the wood find its own shape.

Rasps Up Close: 1. A four-in-one rasp, once called a shoemaker's rasp, combines two rasp and two file surfaces, making it a builders' favorite for general work. The absence of a handle lets it ride comfortably in a tool belt. **2.** A cabinet rasp has uniform teeth that cut quickly. **3.** The irregularly-spaced teeth of a pattern-maker's rasp cut more smoothly—but more slowly—than a cabinet rasp. **4.** A planing rasp is unlikely to clog with chips.

[sawhorses]

All muscle and no ego,

a solid, portable sawhorse is indispensable.

YET IT'S THE ELEGANT WOODWORKER'S WORKBENCH—STATIONARY, thick timbered and loaded with vises—that's revered in books, prized by museums and coveted by collectors. Oddly enough, the carpenter's sawhorse—splay-legged, low and awkwardly portable—is respected only by the person who uses it, and even he sometimes forgets. But not for long. "If they don't arrive on the job first thing," says Tom Silva, "someone will be after the guy who forgot." As a young carpenter, Tom built his own sawhorses, but spruce boards and 2x4s don't last very long after being backed over, kicked around for weeks and left outside in any weather.

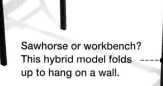

Sawhorse or workbench? This hybrid model folds up to hang on a wall.

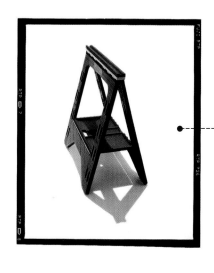

HORSE OF A DIFFERENT COLOR: Made from recycled plastic, this horse has a fold-down shelf for supporting tools. The legs on some models are reinforced with aluminum tubing for extra carrying capacity.
Weight: 12 pounds
Rail length: 30 inches

LIGHT HORSE: Rails and legs are made of 22-gauge galvanized steel; the cross brace is an aircraft-grade cable. A hook-and-loop strap holds folded legs to the rail and doubles as a carrying handle. Self-stabilizing.
Weight: 10 pounds
Rail length: 32½ inches

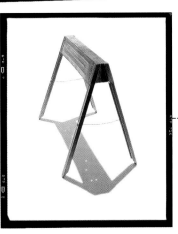

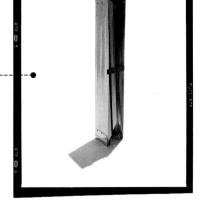

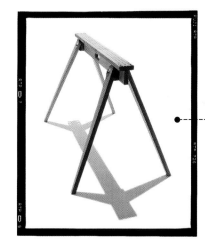

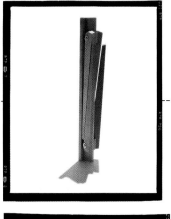

MAPLE MUSTANG: This self-stabilizing maple horse has a weather-resistant finish and a steel folding mechanism. The support rail is slotted to form a carrying handle.
Weight: 16 pounds
Rail length: 43 inches

HIGH HORSE: Tubular steel gets a rust-resistant powder-coated finish on this versatile horse. Each pair of legs can be independently adjusted from 28½ to 38¼ inches high, and can swivel right or left to clear job-site obstructions.
Weight: 22 pounds
Rail length: 32 inches

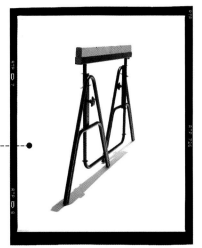

[sawhorses]

a hands-on
interview is what an old-time apprentice faced instead of a written application. If he could build a sturdy pair of fixed-leg sawhorses with reasonable dispatch, he got the job.

"We'd only get two, maybe three jobs out of a horse before we cut it up and tossed it in the trash." Clumsy to load and unload, traditional fixed-leg sawhorses also gobbled up storage space and turned cantankerous when anybody tried to load more than a couple of them into the back of a pickup. That's why Tom now relies only on horses that fold. "A folding sawhorse is a great animal," he says. He steers clear of cheap ones made with 2x4s and flimsy metal brackets: "They're a waste of money. They loosen up and break down and always wobble." Tom's folding horses weigh about 11 pounds each, and their tube-steel legs collapse so neatly that six or eight horses take up as much space in his truck as one of the old nags. Now there's no excuse for leaving them behind.

A sawhorse spends its life showered in sawdust simply because cuts made waist-high are comfortable and efficient. Before using any sawhorse, however, Tom checks its stability. "I set it up, lean on one end and wiggle it. If there's any sway the long way, it's junk." Even a steady horse can topple if loaded unevenly, so Tom centers weight between the horse's legs and provides a solid footing. "Outside," he says, "we put the legs on plywood or lumber so they won't sink in the dirt." On uneven terrain, some horses self-stabilize to eliminate wobble: With a push on the rail, all four legs touch the ground.

Adapting sawhorses to the job is a long-standing practice. Tom protects his with a cheater (a 2x4 screwed to the top rail) that can be replaced after accumulating the inevitable saw kerfs and glue drips. Plumbers hack V-shaped notches into theirs to rein in pipe and keep it from slipping during a cut. A pair of horses and some plywood make a mobile cut-and-paste table for wallpapers. No matter what the trade, one horse seats two for lunch. And as any 7-year-old can tell you, two sawhorses and a blanket make a great hideout.

heirloom horses

FOR FINISH CARPENTER DAN MEYERS, THE QUEST FOR THE PERFECT SAWHORSE BEGAN MORE THAN 40 YEARS AGO, WHEN A FELLOW TRADESMAN LUGGING HORSES THROUGH A DOORWAY PUNCHED A NASTY HOLE IN THE DRYWALL. AS MEYERS REPAIRED THE DAMAGE, HE STARTED THINKING. TWENTY YEARS AND HUNDREDS OF PROTOTYPES LATER, HE FINALLY BUILT A FOLDING WOODEN SAWHORSE THAT SATISFIED HIM; BY 1976, HE'D PATENTED THE DESIGN AND STARTED THE COMPANY HIS DAUGHTER TRACEY NOW RUNS. A MEYERS MAPLE PORTA-FOLD IS STIFF, LIGHT AND SPARE IN THE MANNER OF A SHAKER TABLE. ITS LEGS WON'T SCRATCH A FINISHED FLOOR, AND THEY CAN BE SHORTENED WITHOUT COMPROMISING STRENGTH. HOLES AT EITHER END OF THE RAIL HOLD BENCH DOGS, TURNING THE HORSE INTO A SLENDER WORKBENCH. THE PORTA-FOLD ISN'T EASY TO FABRICATE. "EACH ONE REQUIRES 119 CUTS," TRACEY MEYERS SAYS. NO MAKER OF METAL HORSES CAN MATCH ONE MEYERS SERVICE: "SOMETIMES PEOPLE COME IN WITH WOOD FROM A TREE THEY LOVED. WE CAN USUALLY BE TALKED INTO MAKING A HORSE OUT OF IT." THAT'S HOW MEYERS MADE HIS FIRST CHERRY SAWHORSE.

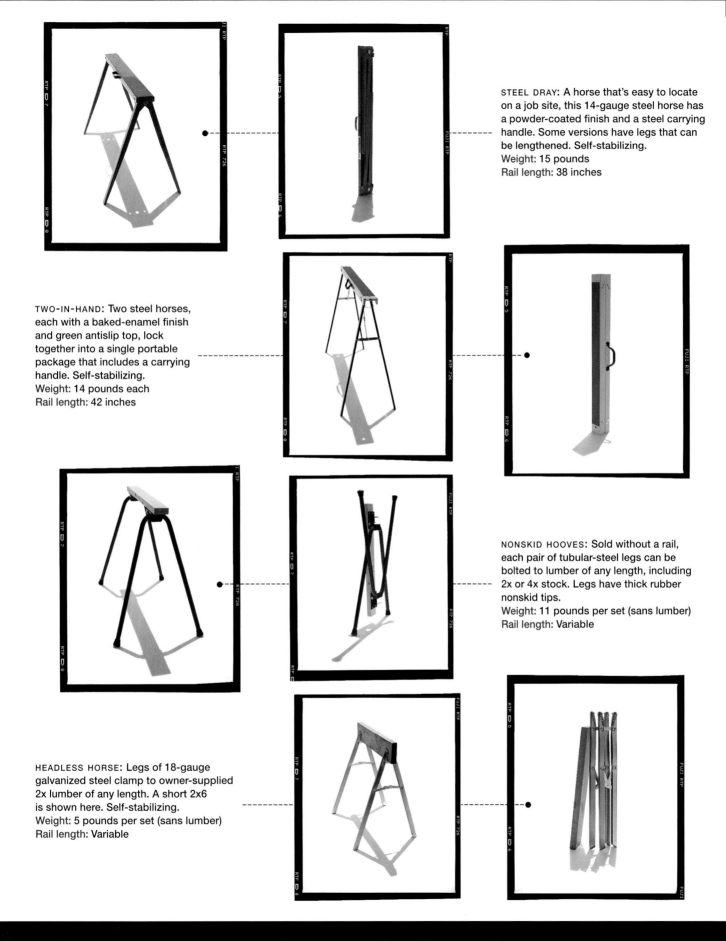

STEEL DRAY: A horse that's easy to locate on a job site, this 14-gauge steel horse has a powder-coated finish and a steel carrying handle. Some versions have legs that can be lengthened. Self-stabilizing.
Weight: 15 pounds
Rail length: 38 inches

TWO-IN-HAND: Two steel horses, each with a baked-enamel finish and green antislip top, lock together into a single portable package that includes a carrying handle. Self-stabilizing.
Weight: 14 pounds each
Rail length: 42 inches

NONSKID HOOVES: Sold without a rail, each pair of tubular-steel legs can be bolted to lumber of any length, including 2x or 4x stock. Legs have thick rubber nonskid tips.
Weight: 11 pounds per set (sans lumber)
Rail length: Variable

HEADLESS HORSE: Legs of 18-gauge galvanized steel clamp to owner-supplied 2x lumber of any length. A short 2x6 is shown here. Self-stabilizing.
Weight: 5 pounds per set (sans lumber)
Rail length: Variable

[staplers]

Staple guns look

like amateur tools, but pros use them a lot.

AND ALTHOUGH THE ACT OF STAPLING IS RELATIVELY SIMPLE, A few caveats apply. Avoid overkill—tacking up a tag-sale poster with $9/16$-inch staples (the longest) will exhaust you. For screening or fabric, the best staple gun is one with a toothed fitting up front to tension the material. Electric guns take the least effort to use and have trigger locks to prevent accidental firings.

Always remember to bring your stapler's make and model number when buying staples, because one size does not fit all. Staples may seem hasty and temporary, says Tom Silva, but people who do real work for a living know how efficient they are. "Don't write off staple guns," he adds, "until you've tiled a ceiling with hammer and nails—then had a long talk with your fingertips and neck." Hammer tackers are unexcelled for placing lightweight staples quickly, making them a favorite for fastening broad expanses of roofing felt and house wrap. Also, hammer tackers have an extralong magazine (the part that holds the supply of staples), which means that a lot more work gets done between reloads.

Electric Stapler/Nailer: An electric model can shoot either staples or the brads (tiny nails) used to install molding. It's canted head is good for tacking in tight spots. An open slot on the magazine shows how many staples remain. **Hammer Tacker:** The pros go for hammer tackers, sturdy tools that place staples quickly and carry plenty of them. A billy-club design like this one is better balanced than older, front-weighted models. **Heavy-Duty Stapler:** This powerful model fires regular and round-crown staples. A cable template on the nose prevents accidental damage to wire insulation. **Cordless Stapler:** Going cordless means adding a heavy battery, but this model holds even the longest standard staples ($9/16$ inch) and can shoot up to 700 of them between rechargings.

Electric Stapler/Nailer

Hammer Tacker

Heavy-Duty Stapler

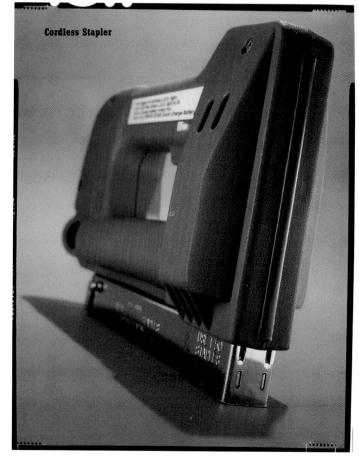

Cordless Stapler

[**tapemeasures**]

AT THEIR MOST BASIC, measuring devices need be nothing more than skinny little sticks of wood on which marks are made. In fact, one way to guard against cutting trim too short or building drawers too big is to avoid using a rule whenever possible. Just hold the piece you need to cut against the space it needs to fit and transfer the measurement directly. But marks on boards don't help builders follow plans or calculate how much wood to buy. Those are jobs that require the standardized increments of tapes and rules.

In early America, rules were generally made in small shops by men who advertised themselves as "mathematical instrument makers." The colonists used various measuring systems which depended on their mother country. In New England, the basic unit was the inch, as laid out on imported copies of a yardstick that England had adopted as its standard. Nevertheless, consistency was an elusive goal. In 1647, Hartford, Connecticut, made it illegal to sell any commodity not measured by an approved device. The town clerk was instructed to "breake or demolishe" any defective rules, such as those made of unseasoned wood.

Rules were often cut from boxwood imported from Turkey—because of the wood's stability and fine grain—then were imprinted with a metal die. The costliest rules were ivory or ebony; the cheapest were maple or steel. Hinges or protective end plates were usually made of brass and sometimes of "German silver," an alloy that despite its name consisted of copper, zinc and nickel.

By the early 1800s, rule-making factories had opened in New York City, Hartford and Charlestown, Massachusetts. In about 1900, a major advance debuted: the first carpenter's compact rule longer than 4 feet. The new 6-foot folding rules were equipped with telescoping or swiveling joints to allow extension in 7- or 8-inch segments. Another big advance was the self-winding metal tape measure of the 1920s. Stanley Rule & Level advertised its Push-Pull model as compact (yet able to measure long distances) and rigid (yet able to flex when

an inch
in the England of 1150 A.D. was defined as the width of a man's thumb. It later became three dry barleycorns laid end to end.

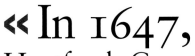

« In 1647, Hartford, Connecticut, made it illegal to sell any commodity not measured by an approved device. »

The tape measure continues to evolve. This one eliminates any doubt about which line belongs to which fraction.

THE 12-INCH MARKS ON THESE THREE NEW TAPE MEASURES VARY BY 1/16 INCH BECAUSE OF VARIATIONS IN THE END TABS. THAT'S WHY IT'S SMART TO USE ONE TAPE THROUGHOUT A PROJECT AND WHY PROS OFTEN BYPASS THE TAB ALTOGETHER ON FINE WORK, MEASURING INSTEAD FROM THE 1-INCH MARK. BUY ONLY TAPE MEASURES THAT HAVE HEFTY TABS.

a question of accuracy

[tape**measures**]

measuring curves). Today, improved versions of these flexible metal rules are the only rules most builders live by, though the standard steel version continues to evolve.

The newest measuring devices link the precision of light and sound waves with the motionless power of electronics. But do these marvels of invention match the elegance of the past? Norm Abram thinks not. He figures that ultrasonic and laser measuring tools are fine for estimating, but he counts a tape with a digital display as a crutch that imperils our mastery of fractions. Instead, he'd rather hold

a box of coiled steel in his hand. He has a few handy tricks for getting the most out of his tape measure.

Ever try to measure inside an opening, such as the distance between two doorjambs, using a tape measure? Textbooks recommend extending the tape until the tip touches the far side and then adding the length of the case (usually 2 or 3 inches; it's often marked). Norm has found, however, that crooked door frames can keep the tape case from fitting into the corner, leading to a measurement that comes up short. Instead, he just tucks the tape's nose tab against one surface and

« In about 1900, a major advance debuted: the first carpenter's rule longer than 4 feet. The new 6-foot folding rules included extension joints. »

WHALER RULES: Rules continued to be handmade when access to commercial products was limited. Nineteenth-century whalers carved these in bone and baleen.

WIZARD RULES: Measuring can be stressful, so some carpenters take rule-aids to their job sites, such as a stick-on calculator or a wipe-off pad. In the 1800s, spit and thumb erased notes made on a case of ass skin.

SCISSOR RULES: Made of ebony and boxwood with brass, these 12-inch two-fold rules also are equipped to be levels, inclinometers, squares and bevels.

Before self-retracting steel tapes, hand-cranked models measured long distances. The Reliable Junior of 1893 has a leather case and pop-out winding handle. The Rival is newer. Both measure 25 feet.

[tapemeasures]

snuggles the other end into the corner and up the opposite jamb. Taking a look at the last place the tape is flat, he eyeballs the width of the gap between that point and the jamb: The length of flat tape plus his estimate of the gap equals the distance between jambs. Norm's practiced eye is very accurate, but even so, he cuts pieces a tad long just in case: "It's easier to trim than to put wood back," he says.

On a framing job, Norm says you can ensure uniform stud or joist spacing by tacking a ¾-inch-long wood scrap to the end of the wall plate. Hook your tape on the scrap so you can mark the location of each stud (16 or 24 inches apart) without having to adjust for zero being at the edge, not the centerline, of the first stud. Put an X after each mark, and you won't end up nailing a whole wall's worth of studs on the wrong side of the line.

Another of Norm's measuring tricks is one that also works nicely with a combination square. To mark a line of any length parallel to the edge of a board, he locks a thumbnail at the desired distance on the rule and holds a pencil against the rule's end, then runs the whole affair down the board. Go ahead: Try that with a handful of barleycorns.

« The newest measuring devices link the precision of light and sound waves with the motionless power of electronics. »

SNEAKY RULES: The secret of the self-winding pocket-size 2-foot rule is a curved steel blade. An early 6-foot zig-zag rule has a sliding extension. It's brother is a yardstick.

TECHNO RULES: A digital tape (top) converts measurements to fractions, decimals or metric units. The laser distance meter (middle) and the smaller sonic tool let users stand still while measuring whole rooms.

CALCULATING RULES: Rules that help with the math, from top: wooden rule with a built-in board-measure table; architect's scales for checking proportions; wire/iron gauges.

The ivory rule is also a penknife; the simple folding rule includes a knife and a retractable pencil. The zig-zag boxwood rule includes a leveling vial.

[**toolbelts**]

IF YOU KNOW WHAT TO LOOK FOR, a carpenter will reveal a lot about himself by the way he carries his tools. A greenhorn carpenter sports a belt bristling with too many tools, and he buckles it tightly around his waist. But a pro keeps his tool belt lightly loaded, loose and slung low on the hips. He knows the contours of the belt so well that he can find anything he needs—a square, a hammer, a handful of nails—without so much as a downward glance. Norm is so attached to his cowhide tool belt that he wears it around the shop instead of grabbing tools off the shelf. "It's so easy to have all you need right at your waist," he says.

« A carpenter will reveal a lot about himself by the way he carries his tools. »

Norm's belt, which has been his faithful hip-side companion for years, has a cotton-web harness with a plastic buckle in back and is easy to put on and take off. The honey-colored pouches, with darkened edges polished by age, have developed the satisfying sags and bulges that make a belt comfortable and give it character. "I like the way the leather feels," Norm says. "Smooth and substantial."

Old habits and eccentricities inevitably determine how a tool belt is used. Norm is right-handed but usually hangs his 16-ounce hammer from a metal loop on his left side. He picked up the habit years ago when the right-hand loop broke on one of his old tool belts. Now, even though he has to reach across his

The shallow outer pockets of Norm's belt hold nails, screws and sandpaper; bigger items go in the deep inside pockets.

body every time he grabs for his hammer, it often ends up in the left-hand loop. "It's a little crazy," he says. Some carpenters shun hammer loops entirely, stuffing the tool deep into a pocket to save the few moments it would take to work it free from a loop.

There is no perfect tool belt. Subtle differences may meet the needs of one workman but not another. Some manufacturers offer special slide-on pouches and tool-holding accessories to match a particular task. If a pouch wears out, it can be tossed without sacrificing the whole belt. Durability, however, is crucial. Tightly stitched seams and rust-resistant rivets at stress points are a must. Canvas pouches are fine, but carpenters in the field need tougher stuff to resist the wear and tear of carrying chisels, nails and other sharp objects. Leather is the traditional choice. Tool belts made of top-grain cowhide—rough on the outside and smooth on the inside—take a beating; they also take a long time to break in. Suede is softer, more supple and easier to break in, but it's thinner and likely to wear out sooner. Cordura, an abrasion-resistant nylon fabric, is light and relatively inexpensive. It won't mildew or crack if it gets wet, but it won't conform to the body.

There are even more options when it comes to choosing the belt's harness: narrow or wide, metal buckles or plastic clips, front or back release. Adjustability can be a problem, especially if the belt will be worn over light clothes in the summer and bulky ones in the winter. Tom Silva's solution? He snipped off the buckle on his tool belt and replaced it with one from a car seat belt.

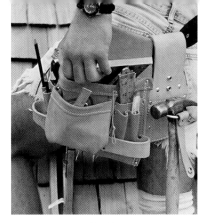

Roofer

Electrician

choosing the right tool belt

THE SIZE AND NUMBER OF POCKETS ON A TOOL BELT ARE LARGELY A MATTER OF TASTE. SOME CARPENTERS PREFER POUCHES THAT SLIDE ALONG THE BELT. OTHERS FEEL MORE COMFORTABLE WITH POUCHES THAT ARE SEWN INTO PLACE SO THEY WON'T SLIP AND SLIDE. IN EITHER CASE, THE POCKETS SHOULD HAVE OPENINGS LARGE ENOUGH TO REACH INTO, AND SMOOTH SEAMS ALONG THE EDGES INSTEAD OF THE BOTTOM, WHERE THEY CAN TRAP NAILS OR OTHER ODDS AND ENDS. AND DEPENDING ON THE TRADE A BELT IS USED FOR, IT CAN SPORT ALL MANNER OF ACCESSORIES.

A GOOD TOOL BELT WILL LAST A PRO AT LEAST THREE OR FOUR YEARS, OR LONGER IF IT IS RE-STITCHED. FOR SOME CARPENTERS, THE REAL PROBLEM COMES IN BREAKING IN A NEW BELT. IT CAN TAKE AT LEAST TWO WEEKS OF STEADY USE FOR STIFF POCKETS TO STRETCH AND FOR LEATHER OR NYLON TO LOSE ITS STORE-BOUGHT SHEEN. INDEED, BRAND-NEW TOOL BELTS ATTRACT SO MUCH ATTENTION THAT SELF-RESPECTING CARPENTERS HAVE BEEN KNOWN TO SCUFF NEW ONES IN THE DIRT AND WEAR THEM AROUND THE HOUSE FOR A FEW DAYS BEFORE BRAVING A JOB SITE. AND WHEN A NEWCOMER SHOWS UP LOOKING FOR WORK, THE FIRST THING THAT'S SCRUTINIZED IS HIS BELT: LIKE A PASSPORT, IT TELLS A LOT ABOUT WHERE HE'S BEEN.

Carpenter

Framer

[utilityknives]

UTILITY KNIVES DIDN'T START OUT AS JACKS-of-all-trades. Stanley Tools' knife #199 was the first (introduced in 1937), but it was heralded as a specialized cutter for fiberboard. The 199 had a cast-aluminum handle with antislip checkering—like that on period gunstocks—and a rigid blade that permitted accurate cutting. Users soon found it could slice roofing felt, insulation and even sheet tin in a pinch, so it was promoted to "trimming knife" in the company's 1939 catalog.

Fifteen years later, after 199s cut their way through thousands of dungaree pockets, Stanley introduced a retractable-blade model. Over the years, utility, or "razor" knives have acquired a degree of sophistication far beyond the 199's humble beginnings.

There are knives with blade-storing handles, tool-free blade changing, brightly colored "designer" casings and cocked handgrips for comfort and leverage. The latest

①

« Over the years, utility knives have acquired a degree of sophistication far beyond their humble beginnings. **»**

a scored blade *can be snapped off in a moment to expose a fresh edge whenever cutting slows down, reducing the expense of blade replacement.*

A Gallery Of Utility Knives: 1. Loosening the center button allows the housing to hinge open without the need for a screwdriver. 2. The original utility knife is compact and simple with a textured handle for a secure grip. Access to the blade storage compartment requires a screwdriver. 3. This retractable-blade knife has a protective knuckle-duster grip and a blade storage compartment. 4. The 19-degree bend in this handle means more power for each cut, and the bright color makes it easy to find in a toolbox. Like most utility knives, this one will accept a variety of blades, including this notching blade.

versions have locking mechanisms that keep retractable blades from wobbling. Despite the advances, plenty of renovators clamor for the old classic 199, which is still manufactured though it's now called model 10-209.

Whatever the shape, a utility knife isn't just a cutup. Contractors with a passion for accuracy use it as an ultraprecise pencil for such tasks as scribing cut lines and locating

hinge leaves. Another benefit of using a blade instead of a pencil in such cases is that the scored layout line lessens the chance that subsequent chisel work will stray outside the layout. A deeply scored line reduces chipping too. Of course, a sharp utility knife is also the tool that pros reach for when less-accurate marking is needed: There's nothing better for quickly whittling down a carpenter's pencil.

[**workbenches**]

STUCK AT HOME WITH the flu, most kids would end up in front of the television. Not Norm Abram. As a child, the master carpenter once spent the better part of a day busily carving his initials into the mahogany headboard of his parents' bed. A woodworker was born. Somewhat later, at a small homemade workbench in his basement, he worked on model cars and glued up furnishings for his sister's playhouse. After college, Norm started a construction company, which specialized in restoration. To make cabinets for his clients and to cut and mill trim for windows and doors, he rigged on-site workbenches from sawhorses and plywood. He started using his current bench about 12 years ago. The difference between it and field-built benches was a revelation. "Nothing comes close to this in the field," he says, thumping the top of his bench. "I don't know how I managed without it."

Ground zero for all manner of pounding, pummeling, pushing and pulling, a workbench must be strong. The base should be broad with trestles or braces to keep the bench from racking, and the joints should be tight— mortise and tenon are best. Most important, the top should be made from close-grained wood, such as maple, birch or beech, to add weight (Norm's bench is a hefty 300 pounds) and keep the bench from skittering and bouncing while a board is planed or dovetails are cut. A dense wood is more dimensionally stable than a soft one; the top won't shift

Getting To Know A Workbench: Hundreds of accessories are available for workbenches, but Norm prefers to keep things simple. Off-the-shelf clamps are his accessory of choice. He uses them to secure a tabletop section (above) while cutting slots in the edge with a biscuit joiner. **The Bench Dogs:** Norm prefers square bench dogs for their holding power. They're less likely than round dogs to indent wood. **The Face Vise:** Wood jaws, shown here, should be wide to grip all manner of objects. A sliding lever-handle allows one-handed adjustments. **The Bench Top:** A well-made bench is a beautiful piece of furniture. A few cuts from a stray blade give it character, but Norm uses a sheet of cellulose fiberboard to protect the top during messy work such as gluing up projects. **The Workstation:** A workbench is a tool; it's just bigger than most others. It is also a particularly effective workstation for a router or an orbital sander. Here, Norm uses a section of rubber mesh (like the mats that keep area rugs from slipping) to anchor a board while he sands it.

The Bench Dogs

The Face Vise

The Bench Top

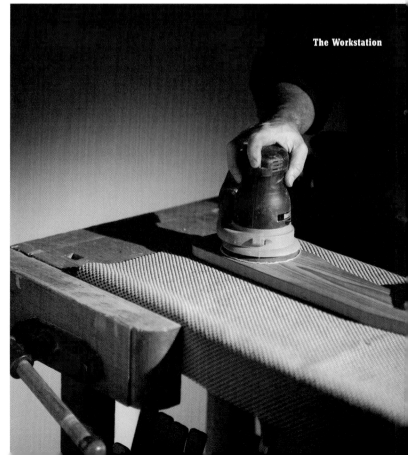

The Workstation

[workbenches]

This Canadian bench, available in kits or fully assembled, features a maple top, a twin-screw vise and a sturdy trestle base.

Building a bench is a good first project for novice woodworkers. This bench incorporates several different types of joinery including dadoes and rabbets.

Built for site work, the top of this minibench opens to form a vise or closes to create a work surface. The collapsible frame includes a step to give the bench stability.

This birch-topped bench isn't as beefy as professional models but includes plenty of storage space in the base.

WHETHER YOU PLAN TO BUY A BENCH OR BUILD ONE, TRY IT ON FOR SIZE FIRST. A BENCH SHOULD BE TALL ENOUGH TO PREVENT BACKACHES AND LOW ENOUGH TO PROVIDE LEVERAGE. SELECT THE LARGEST WORKBENCH YOUR SPACE CAN HOLD, BECAUSE—LIKE A DESK OR A KITCHEN TABLE—IT WILL QUICKLY FILL WITH STUFF.

choosing a workbench

« Select the largest bench your work area can hold, because—like a desk or a kitchen table—it will quickly fill with stuff. »

around as much with changes in humidity. And a good, thick top can be planed if it's marred. Some woodworkers spend more time sanding and oiling a bench top than working on it, but Norm is not among them. After all, a good workbench may look like a fine piece of furniture, but it's meant to be used.

There are plenty of specialized stops, jigs and clamps for benches, and some woodworkers swear by them. But Norm, ever practical, eschews the fancy gewgaws and keeps his workbench simple. A good vise, some bench dogs and some standard clamps are usually all he needs. Vises keep wood from moving as it is worked; without them, a workbench is little more than a glorified table. One debate that never fails to stir passions among woodworkers is over what type of vise works best. Wood jaws won't leave marks on the project being clamped, and wood screw mechanisms are, well, traditional. Norm prefers wood faces with metal screw mechanisms, however, because metal is stronger and less subject to wear. A pair of vises—a face vise that opens at the front of the bench and a tail vise that opens at the end—offer maximum flexibility.

Bench dogs help to hold large pieces of stock on the workbench. The dogs slip into holes in the work surface and serve as backstops as the tail vise supplies clamping pressure. The best type of bench dog is another topic debated endlessly. Metal dogs don't break like wooden ones but are more expensive, and some can mar the edges of stock. Round dogs permit clamping from any angle, but square ones offer better holding power because of their greater contact area.

There's no debate about clamps, though: Just about any woodworker would agree that more is better. Norm gets a lot of mileage out of spring clamps (the kind that can be opened with one hand). Two orderly rows of the critters cling to the rails beneath his bench, unobtrusive but readily accessible. Norm uses other clamps as needed, of course, but his team of a bench vise and bench dog are generally up to any clamping challenge.

norm's first
workbench was probably just like yours: one of those toys children pound on to force small pegs into round or square holes.

[worklights]

WHEN A PROJECT TAKES YOU INTO THE DARKER recesses of your house, a work light becomes your best friend. Flashlights offer the ultimate in portable brightening, and today's torches have all sorts of handy features, including flex necks, magnetic bases, swivel heads, long-life rechargeable battery packs and adjustable light beams. But for long-term lighting, you'll want something you can plug in.

"Trouble lights" are the old standbys found in workshops and garages. Some newer models, in addition to having plastic cages and comfortable handles, double as an extension cord by including an extra outlet in the handle.

Descended from the sleek, chrome-plated jobs used by doctors to peer into ears and down throats, these plastic models have spring clips that grab onto pockets, belts and hat brims for convenience in close quarters.

With up to 500 watts of lighting power, there's nothing brighter than halogen lamps. But user beware: They generate enough heat to burn skin and combust sawdust, and they should be covered with a wire guard and a glass faceplate. Even when cool, the bulb should never be touched, because skin oil can trigger an explosive bulb failure.

Hanging lights haven't changed much over time, but they've changed for the better. Old-style metal cages that rust and dent have given way to corrosion-proof plastic guards that don't conduct electricity. Durable-use incandescent bulbs can be added to almost any trouble light; they'll hold up better against job-site abuse. Some fluorescent work lights have neither cord nor batteries. These lights keep costs low and convenience high by connecting directly to an extension cord. The slim-line shape and cool glow reach even the least accessible places, making them just right for quick forays into the crawl-space underworld.

A light with a rechargeable battery delivers freedom from the cord as well as versatility: The light features a neck that can swing up to 120 degrees.

Fluorescent models provide cool light without glare. This model has no cord. It simply plugs into whatever extension cord you supply.

The ribbing of these flex-necked lights enables them to cling like giant flexible ties to anything handy. Some use the same rechargeable batteries as heavy-duty cordless tools; other lights have two beam options (pencil and flood).

Halogen lights are ideal indoors when there's a wall to paint or some drywall to tape—the intense, raking light creates shadows that expose every flaw. A single halogen can illuminate an entire room.

For probing attics, basements and other nooks and crannies, a basic flashlight is helpful, but you can do better than the basic model. The red light has a ratchet head that directs light where you need it, while the yellow light is a recharge-able unit that can stand up all by itself.

* * *
CREDITS

AUTHORS: Peter Edmonston (Work Lights), Mark Feirer (Sawhorses), Jeanne Huber (Block Planes, Hand Scrapers, Tape Measures) Peter Jensen (Paintbrushes), John Kelsey (Chisels, Pliers), Bill Marsano (Multi-Tools, Utility Knives), James Morgan (Ladders), Stephen L. Petranek (Hammers, Levels), William Sampson (Hacksaws, Staplers), Wendy Talarico (Pipe Clamps, Tool Belts, Workbenches) and Jeff Taylor (Combination Squares, Drywall Trowels, Handsaws, Mechanical Screwdrivers, Nail Pullers, Paint Scrapers, Plumb Bobs).

PHOTOGRAPHERS: Greg Anthon, David Barry, David Bartolomi, Dan Borris, Chris Buck, Jim Cooper, Anthony Cotsifas, Michael Grimm, Darrin Hadded, Spencer Jones, Keller & Keller, Kristine Larsen, Marko Lavrisha, Joshua McHugh, Martin Mistretta, Daniel Moss, Michael Myers, Benjamin Oliver, Erik Rank, Rosa & Rosa, Greg Slater (Workbook Co/Op Stock), Ted & Debbie, Dan Vermillion, Garry Wade, Bill White, Kevin Wilkes and James Wojcik. Additional photographs courtesy of Eazypower Corp. and Taka.

ILLUSTRATIONS: Bob Hambly and Clancy Gibson

THIS OLD HOUSE BOOKS
EDITOR: Mark Feirer
DESIGN DIRECTOR: Matthew Drace
ART DIRECTOR: Delgis Canahuate
PROJECT COORDINATOR: Miriam Silver
PRODUCTION DIRECTOR: Denise Clappi
ART ASSOCIATE: Matthew Bates
PRODUCTION ASSOCIATE: Donna Robinson
COPY EDITORS: Elena Kornbluth and Rebecca Reisner
PROOFREADER: Eric Page

PUBLISHER, BOOKS: Andrew McColough

VICE PRESIDENT, CONSUMER MARKETING: Greg Harris

SPECIAL THANKS TO: Norm Abram, Steve Thomas, Tom Silva, Richard Trethewey, Bruce Irving and Russell Morash at the show; Karen Johnson and Peter McGhee at WGBH; Stephen Petranek and Eric Thorkilsen at *This Old House* magazine; Anthony Wendling and Ray Galante at Applied Graphics Technology; and interns Nataly Kolesnikova and Nino Kartozia.

Funding for *This Old House* on public television is provided by State Farm Insurance Companies, Ace Hardware Corporation and The Minwax & Krylon Brands.

« The timeworn surface of a favored tool reminds us of what the craftsman has accomplished. »